# VOYA's Five-Foot Bookshelf

## Essential Books for Professionals Who Serve Teens, 2000 through 2012

VOYA Magazine Editors

VOYA Press

an imprint of E L Kurdyla Publishing, LLC

Bowie, Maryland

ISBN 978-1-61751-010-6

Copyright © 2013

Published by VOYA Press, an imprint of E L Kurdyla Publishing LLC

LCCN: 2012935475

The paper used in this publication meets the minimum requirements of the American National Standard for Information Sciences-Permanence of Paper for Printed Materials, ANSI Z39.48-1992.

Printed in the United States of America

# Introduction

Each October VOYA presents Extending the Five-Foot Bookshelf, an annotated list of the professional books for school and public librarians and media specialists published in the previous year that received the best reviews in VOYA. The compilers of the annual lists reread all the professional book reviews in VOYA of the previous year, examine many of the books, and select the best for the list following the criteria listed below.

Susan Rosenzweig, a former school librarian and library educator, inaugurated The Five-Foot Bookshelf in 1997, providing a list of fifteen essential titles dating back to 1990. VOYA reviewer and Professor Hilary S. Crew assumed the responsibility in 2001, followed by VOYA cofounder Mary K. Chelton in 2003, and then former VOYA editor Cathi Dunn MacRae in 2006. David Loertscher, co-editor of Teacher Librarian, compiled the lists for 2007 and 2008, and RoseMary Honnold, editor-in-chief of VOYA compiled the 2009 through 2012 lists.

This compilation of professional titles for 2000 through 2012 represents the best resources for young adult librarianship in the twenty-first century. These titles impressed our reviewers, and most became essential professional resources for our readers. They are presented here with the full original reviews.

## Five-Foot Bookshelf Criteria

The intent of this professional reading list is to "identify books that increase our understanding of teenagers and how to serve them, serve as an inspiration to youth workers, and/ or add to our knowledge of the field." (VOYA October 1997, p. 225) These books are so essential that is would be difficult to serve teens without having read them.

## Included:

- Professional books for both public and school librarians addressing policy issues, evaluation, public relations, advocacy, intellectual freedom, youth participation, programming, new research findings, education, literacy, technology, and similar topics.

- Books from other disciplines on adolescent development; current youth issues; racial, ethnic, and gender issues; teen culture; and youth development (including such topics as mentoring, dropout prevention, and delinquency prevention).

## Excluded:

- Collection development tools, bibliographies, and lists of recommended books for young adults.
- Biographies or critiques of authors.
- Books designed as textbooks in library or education courses.
- Resource guides to websites, reference materials, etc.

# Five-Foot Bookshelf
## 2000 through 2012

Adams, Helen R. **Ensuring Intellectual Freedom and Access to Information in the School Library Media Program**. Libraries Unlimited, 2008. 254p. $40 Trade pb. 978-1-59158-539-8. Index. Source Notes. Further Reading. **VOYA** April 2009.

This excellent, comprehensive, and up-to-date treatment of intellectual freedom, with an introduction by library school professor and author Dianne McAfee Hopkins, is an indispensable work for school library media specialists in all kinds of schools, including international and private schools. For example, the chapter on the First Amendment and minors' right to read, view, and access materials on the Internet clarifies the differences on how restrictions might be applied according to whether students are in public or private school or in school or public libraries. Emphasis is placed on the impact of the First Amendment and on federal and state legislation and court cases with which school library media specialists and school administrators should be familiar. Adams's broad approach to intellectual freedom is evident in chapters on the selection of materials, access to library materials for students with disabilities, "The Right to Read," privacy, challenges to materials, Internet access, and advocacy. Chapters include abundant strategies and resources.

Especially relevant are the candid voices of professionals who bring their experiences and expertise to bear on issues such as filtering and challenges, self-censorship, social networking, and parents' concerns about individual choice of reading materials. Current topics include the impact of technology on privacy including identification technology for automation, the use of surveillance cameras, and issues regarding computerized reading programs. Appendixes include three authors' responses to censorship, "Right to Read Lesson Plans," as well as intellectual freedom documents. The coverage and level of discussion make this work highly useful for academic and professional development purposes.—Hilary Crew.

Agosto, Denise E., and June Abbas, Eds. **Teens, Libraries, and Social Networking: What Librarians Need to Know**. Libraries Unlimited, 2011. 190p. $40 Oversize pb. 978-1-59884-575-4. Index. **VOYA** October 2011.

This professional reference guide is the go-to source for information about using social networking to connect to young adults in a public library setting. The editors open the book with research that shows how libraries are actually using social networking sites today and how teenagers use those same technologies. They then describe the positive impact social networking can have on teenagers. Next, is a description of several social networking options. They then move into a discussion of safety concerns and laws associated with social networking. The next few chapters describe some various social networking platforms and how to use them in teen library services. Finally, the authors describe Charlotte Mecklenburg Library's development and use of social networking in their branches, and they end with an overview of the book's main points.

The authors do an outstanding job of basing their content on studies that show actual usage of social networking by libraries and by teenagers, showing the implications of those findings for libraries, and making recommendations to libraries based on that research. This reference guide will be useful to librarians seeking evidence to support the use of social networking with young adults in their libraries; those interested in the range of social networking sites currently available; and those looking for a few ideas on how to use social networking tools in their young adult programs. Although the book is solid, it would be nice to see more examples of programming ideas along with the particulars of how to run them.—C. Clark.

**American Indian Stereotypes in the World of Children: A Reader and Bibliography**, Second Edition. Arlene Hirschfelder, Paulette Fairbanks Molin, and Yvonne Wakim, Eds. Scarecrow, 1999. 384p. $44.55 Trade pb. 978-0-8108-3613-6. Index. Illus. Biblio. **VOYA** June 2000.

This volume presents a collection of challenging articles detailing uses and abuses of Native American symbols, images, ideas, and stories that are directed at youth in the mass media. Toys, cartoons, textbooks, general reading, media portrayals, sports logos, nicknames, and more are discussed in stand-alone articles. Continually faced with stereotypes and offensive portrayals, Native children have difficulties developing strong, positive self images. Chilling accounts given by children show just how important this issue is, emphasizing that it is not possible to start teaching too early. Topics addressed include the offensive terms in alphabet books, this work, the depiction of animals dressed in Native costumes, and poorly planned class assignments. In updating the earlier edition, this work adds information that is more recent as well as a wealth of article, book, and Web site bibliographical references.

Every time librarians purchase materials for their collections that have negative or inaccurate representations of Native Americans, more youth are endangered. The recent debates about Rinaldi's **My Heart is on the Ground** (Scholastic, 1999/**VOYA** October 1999) show how important these issues are for readers of all ages today. Through these articles, librarians and teachers can better understand what is offensive and how to avoid perpetuating hurtful stereotypes and images with all children. This important title should be required reading for all librarians, especially those in collection development, as well as educators. For more information about selecting accurate, affirming materials, see **Through Indian Eyes** (Slapin and Seale, 1998) and the Oyate Web site, *http://www. oyate.org.*--Mary B. McCarthy.

Anderson, Sheila B. **Extreme Teens: Library Services to Nontraditional Young Adults**. Libraries Unlimited, 2005. 176p. $38 Trade pb. 978-1-59158-170-3. Index. Biblio. Source Notes. Further Reading. VOYA April 2006.

Public library director and longtime teen and teen services advocate Anderson offers insight and advice on planning and providing effective service to young adults who are outside the mainstream. She identifies a broad spectrum of descriptors as falling into her term "extreme," including homeless youth, those learning English, pregnant and parenting teens, high school dropouts, teens enrolled simultaneously in both high school and college classes, teens in foster care, and emancipated minors. Because this series is intended to give professionals practical guidance, Anderson does not spend time on analyzing the hows involved in teens becoming members of any of her "extreme" categories, but instead emphasizes ways to reach them and supply them with excellent information services. She describes real programs in a variety of public library settings; presents reading lists of young adult literature, professional literature, and pertinent organizations; and ends with a rousing chapter of public relations projects that a library would want to borrow to reach any and all groups of prospective users, including but not limited to extreme teens.

Administrators, as well as youth-serving library staff, should read this title in order to get a realistic overview of the diversity of circumstances library services need to address when trying to reach the teen demographic.-Francisca Goldsmith.

Aronson, Marc. **Beyond the Pale: New Essays for a New Era**. Scarecrow Press, 2003. 145p. $41.25. 978-0-8108-4638-8. Index. Source Notes. **VOYA** August 2004.

Aronson justifies his criticism of topics ranging from identity-based awards to nonfiction relegated as *publishing's* neglected stepchild with the simple statement, "[A] book a teenager should read is any book." The odd title acknowledges the author's father, a Jew saddled by cultural restrictions and living in a settlement labeled The Pale, who journeys to Moscow in the early twentieth century and challenges rules by viewing impressionistic artwork that opened his mind. Aronson suggests that the publishing industry also needs to challenge accepted thinking in three areas: the purpose of multicultural awards, how publishers fail in promoting books for male teens, and how novels dripping with angst are not meant for all young adults. Combining written essays with speech transcripts, Aronson's words will prompt discussion about the direction of young adult literature, and his thoughts will resound throughout the library field. Adopting the controversial stance that multicultural awards limit readers, Aronson suggests doing away with or adjusting such tributes as the Coretta Scott King and Pura Belpré awards, contending that these nationally recognized achievements influence readers to read only from that category, thus impeding multicultural goals. Suggesting that modern male teens need but have little opportunity to tinker with machinery (leading to guys' video game fascination as an outlet), Aronson states that libraries and publishers fail miserably to provide how-to nonfiction titles for teens. Essays submitted by notable professionals responding to the author's viewpoints balance the book's tone. Controversial? Yes. Interesting? Yes. Is it a must-read for professionals working with young adults? A definite yes.—Rollie Welch.

Aronson, Marc. **Exploding the Myths: The Truth about Teenagers and Reading**. Scarecrow Press, 2001. 145p. $40.70. 978-0-8108-3904-5. Index. **VOYA** June 2001.

Ushered in with a thoughtful foreword by author Bruce Brooks, this provocative collection of speeches and previously published essays challenges those who work with teenagers and their reading to shift paradigms, shatter illusions, and examine the essence of young adult literature. Aronson, author and editor of young adult books, begins with a heartfelt declaration that, despite predictions to the contrary, YA literature is truly alive and well. Then he explores the "borderlines and defining characteristics" of YA literature, its multicultural facets and perspectives, its lack of substantial critical reviews, and the role of adult books for teens. Two fascinating chapters deal with Aronson's experiences at a 1997 international conferences on teenagers and reading in Rome (see **VOYA**, *Soapbox*, June 1998, and *YA 101*, October and December 1998). First, he focuses on the national and cultural differences that affect teen literature, then describes YA publishing in American and encourages more global elements within it. An examination of art in YA literature presents an interesting and ultimately effective comparison to the ballet *Giselle*, through which the coming-of-age journey is exemplified. Realism versus moralism, the awesome power of words in YA literature, and misconceptions fostered about teenagers are additional topics addressed. A chapter on the new Printz Award is actually an analysis of how YA books are judged and reviewed, with ratings by quality and popularity. Aronson carefully explains why he feels popularity evaluations are "intellectually indefensible" and "a stealth term disguising adult bias." The final essay deals with YA books that "grapple with a world in upheaval," followed by an introspective interview with author Jacqueline Woodson.

Librarians, teacher, students and professors of adolescent literature, publishers, editors and authors need to read and contemplate this worthy companion to Michael Cart's excellent **From Romance to Realism: 50 Years of Growth and Change in Young Adult Literature** (HarperCollins, 1996).—Diane P. Tuccillo.

Auguste, Margaret. **VOYA's Guide to Intellectual Freedom for Teens**. VOYA Press, 2012. 187p. $40. 978-1-61751-007-6.

**VOYA's Guide to Intellectual Freedom for Teens** was not reviewed in VOYA.

Beers, Kylene. **When Kids Can't Read: What Teachers Can Do: A Guide for Teachers 6 - 12**. Heinemann, 2003. 368p. $40.63 Trade pb. 978-0-86709-519-7. **VOYA** August 2003.

This newest book by the author of **Into Focus: Understanding and Creating Middle School Readers** (Christopher Gordon, 1998/**VOYA** December 1998) should be required reading for all current English teachers and those preparing for the profession. It is the culmination of Beers's twenty-three years in the classroom, about half of which had been spent working specifically with struggling readers. Most secondary English teachers do not plan to teach kids how to read; they expect to assign classic novels and discuss literature. Beers held this ideal as she began her first teaching assignment, but she was quickly disillusioned. Many of her students hated to read, and a large number of them could not read. Her inability that first year to help one student named George was the catalyst by which she became an advocate for struggling readers.

Each of the fifteen chapters begins and ends with a note to George, which adds a poignant tone to the author's message. Beers provides teaching strategies and activities, along with the rationale behind them. While admitting that it takes time, practice, and dedication, she never asks teachers to do anything that she has not already tested herself. Worth mentioning is Beers's underlying premise that all readers are struggling in some way. The key is to become an independent struggling reader, one who possesses the tools to meet the challenge of any type of text. Not only can struggling readers improve but good readers can as well. As this reviewer, also a high school English teacher of twenty-three years, discovered, Beers offers real answers rather than just educational theories.—Kim Zack.

Berger, Pam, and Sally Trexler. **Choosing Web 2.0 Tools for Learning and Teaching in a Digital World**. Libraries Unlimited, 2010. 175p. $40 Trade pb. 978-1-59158-706-4. Glossary. Appendix. Index. Illus. Photos. Charts. **VOYA** August 2010.

As a guide for incorporating digital literacy into the library and classroom curriculum, the text begins with an overview of the components of Web 2.0 and examines learning in the twenty-first century. One chapter outlines efficient use of the Web through effective searches, as well as the organization of information through social bookmarking. Another chapter addresses time and personal management—skills that are essential to student success— which can be supported through personal information spaces and online organizers. "Content Collaboration" addresses the use of Wiki pages, course blogs, and other collaboration tools to encourage student connection both inside and outside the classroom or library. The book uncovers a number of other useful devices as well and encourages the incorporation and instruction of a multitude of digital tools to heighten student engagement and experiential learning.

This guide comes at a crucial time, as technology has found a permanent and essential place in education, and "teacher librarians, as information and communication specialists, must lead change in their buildings or face irrelevancy." For students, the Web is a social, creative, educational, and recreational site of learning and play. It is a very real focus in their lives, and thus it must become a tool in education as well. This guide offers a plethora of ideas for incorporating digital learning into schools in an accessible and reader-friendly manner. This is an excellent tool for any educator interested in enriching students' education through digital literacy.—Courtney Huse Wika.

Bernier, Anthony. **VOYA's YA Spaces of Your Dreams Collection**. VOYA Press, 2012. 221p. $50. 978-1-61751-011-3.

    **VOYA's YA Spaces of Your Dreams Collection** was not reviewed in VOYA.

Bolan, Kimberly. **Teen Spaces: The Step-by-Step Library Makeover**. ALA Editions, 2009. 225p. $50 Trade pb. 978-0-8389-0969-0. Index. Illus. Photos. Charts. Biblio. Source Notes. Further Reading. Appendix. **VOYA** April 2009.

    Opinions have always been split about teen spaces. Teen librarians feel a space that encourages teenagers to visit the library is essential. Other library employees view the same space as frivolous. To allow the frivolous camp to see the light, Bolan's work is an essential purchase, especially during the current economic downturn. In this second edition, teen input is emphasized, but a knee-jerk "gimmee" list wisely is discouraged. Bolan emphasizes to "do your homework" before any implementation of a teen space begins. The key is to understand your market. She encourages readers to balance teen needs and wants before meeting with designers and decorators. Refreshingly the "Long-Term Promotion" chapter includes the teen collection as a major asset of a teen space. This chapter is also chockfull of cool suggestions such as Yamaha keyboards, video editing, and digital cameras. Teen librarians are well aware of the hook of technology, and this chapter is an outstanding example of justifying inclusion of techie gadgets that may be pricey.

    The text is very readable, with a tone that encourages readers to take a look at their own situation. It avoids being preachy or pretentious by only outlining top teen spaces that perhaps have set the bar too high for most libraries. Bolan has wisely broken up the text by Tip Boxes (Ask local hardware stores to donate cans of clearance paint) and photographs of a wide variety of teen spaces around the United States. One page has photos of Loudonville, New York, juxtaposed with an area in Palos Verdes, California. Back matter is especially well done. The limitless retail world of the Internet has been organized into an up-to-date appendix with sections such as Technology, Design Services, Flooring and Ceilings, and Collection Development. Another appendix lists libraries currently using teen spaces. A chart includes each library's Web site, the teen space's square footage, and the estimated population served by the library. This unique information makes this professional title one of the more useful works in print for both novice and experienced librarians. Slide this one under your supervisor's door with post-it notes marking key pages. Results will follow.—Rollie Welch.

Booth, Char. **Reflective Teaching, Effective Learning: Instructional Literacy for Library Educators**. ALA Editions, 2011. 208p. $60. Oversize pb. 978-0-8389-1052-8. Index. Source Notes. Appendix. Glossary. Illus. Charts. Further Reading. **VOYA** August 2011.

    "If I was called to librarianship, I was thrown into teaching." So begins the introductory chapter of this exceptional guide to teaching in the library environment, and for so many of us, truer words were never spoken. Teaching is frequently an afterthought in library education programs, and it can be frustrating and demoralizing to face classes—whether virtual or in person—feeling that one lacks the knowledge and confidence to teach effectively. And while this book is a godsend to novice teachers, even seasoned practitioners who are looking for fresh approaches will benefit from its guidance. What readers will not find here: canned lesson plans, scripted tutorials, or step-by-step activities. What they will find: an in-depth discussion of every aspect of instructional literacy combined with a set of strategies that will help librarians create effective instruction that can be adapted for any type of situation, be it a quick online tutorial or a full semester class. Each brief chapter ends with a summary and reflection points. The author includes planning templates, recommendations for further reading that are current and comprehensive, and a glossary of key terms.

Although this book is targeted to academic librarians, it will be a valuable professional resource for librarians in any setting who want to continuously challenge themselves to create engaging and effective learning experiences.—Jane Harper.

Booth, David. **Reading Doesn't Matter Anymore: A New Way to Look at Reading**. Pembroke/Stenhouse, 2006. 176p. $16 Trade pb. 978-1-57110-492-2. Further Reading. **VOYA** August 2007.

Renowned Canadian professor emeritus Booth maintains that educators and others must redefine meanings and methodologies of literacy and reading education to meet contemporary students' needs and interests in this scholarly yet exceptionally readable text. Complex definitions and theory are followed by pointed, witty, personal examples from the author, creating a text appearing far less academic than actually written. Chapters succinctly discuss viewing and teaching literacy and reading, with a crucial statement of reading being more than novels: it is the Internet, e-mail, comics, text-messaging, and more, with the epilogues 101 Literacy Events providing classroom practices. An overall premise for encouraging and expanding reading and literacy is to have teachers and students reading relevant texts, writing real thoughts, and sharing authentic feelings while valuing the learning involved in doing so.

Readers knowledgeable of best practices yet finding them compromised by heightened assessment and other demands will gobble this text, thrilled by its validation. Booth discusses common practices such as skill and drill, spelling tests, worksheets, separating reading and writing, classics only, teacher-directed interpretation and critique, book reports, and more—and then skewers them by showing their ineffectiveness regarding literacy. Thoughtful and pithy statements include, "Do you really want a ten-year-old boy to have the same literary taste as a forty-year-old divorced teacher?" when considering ill-fitting novel choices. Booth provocatively asks, "What role does school play in determining the roles that books will hold in young people's lives? Any?" Although a must-have for literacy educators, this text would most benefit educational critics and policy-makers.—Lisa Hazlett.

Booth, Heather. **Serving Teens Through Readers' Advisory**. ALA Editions, 2007. 159p. $47 Trade pb. 978-08389-0930-0. Glossary. Index. Charts. Biblio. Source Notes. Chronology. Appendix. **VOYA** October 2007.

Booth provides a fantastic professional-development book for youth and teen services librarians. This excellently organized and researched book offers the basics of readers' advisory (RA) service and shows how easily and efficiently it can be adapted for work with teen patrons. She stresses the absolute importance of not making judgments about reading choices with teens because librarians are trained not to do so with adult patrons. Uniquely teen-patron issues are homework readers' advisory help and working with the dual-action RA interview when teens are with parents. RA sources, both print and electronic, are summarized and evaluated along with steps for all staff, even those not directly assigned to work with teen patrons, to become knowledgeable about young adult literature. Reading plans, speed reading, note taking, booklists, and annotation skills are covered. A brief history of readers' advisory service and teen reading as well as their relationships to libraries is detailed. Popular author lists and Sure Bets lists are in the very helpful appendixes, especially for those new to YA services and YA literature.

This must-have purchase for professional collections should be mandatory reading for all staff members who work directly with teens and any others who have daily contact with teen patrons. An easy-to-use and helpful glossary and index make this resource perfect for both the novice and experienced librarian. This essential guide provides skills, sources, and tools for providing fabulous readers' advisory service to teens.-Karen Sykeny.

Braun, Linda W. **Technically Involved: Technology-Based Youth Participation Activities for Your Library**. ALA Editions, 2003. 160p. $30 Trade pb. 978-0-8389-0861-7. Index. Charts. Source Notes. Appendix. **VOYA** June 2004.

Braun, author of the helpful **Teens.library** (ALA, 2002/ **VOYA** August 2002), creates another resource for those who work with teens and want to capture and focus the energy and enthusiasm of youth. Here she stresses the importance of ensuring that teen volunteers have true input and control over their involvement with library programs and services, and she tries to instill the idea that just showing up for programs or volunteer time does not indicate true youth participation. Braun provides concise tips and strategies for working with teens and for developing youth participation programs where teens are in charge from start to finish and librarians act only as guides or advisors. In addition, she relates how crucial it is to have the absolute support and understanding of all public service, management, and technology staff, while suggesting ideas on how to accomplish and gain this support. The book is full of lists, charts, and tables, as well as some outlines for possible projects for implementing successful teen participation programs that focus on technology issues, such as e-mail newsletters, online library tour guides, and wireless service connections in teen areas. Especially nice is the section discussing projects concerning literacy issues by creating blogs or teen guides.

This book is a wonderful and insightful guide that provides skills and tools for creating an active, successful, and fulfilling cooperation for both teens and librarians. Its basic organization for chapters begins with lists of central ideas and skills for teens to accomplish, a more in-depth explanation of the list, and then a detailed "how-to" section for some sample projects.-Karen Sykeny.

Braun, Linda W. **Teens, Technology, and Literacy: Or, Why Bad Grammar Isn't Always Bad**. Libraries Unlimited, 2007. 128p. $30 Trade pb. 978-1-59158-368-4. Index. Photos. Source Notes. Appendix. **VOYA** October 2007.

Braun does educators, especially librarians, a great service by writing this book. Literacy has traditionally been defined within the parameters of reading and writing; Braun shows that every type of technology used by teens for communication, school-work, and leisure reinforces and hones literacy skills. Clear, concise, and intelligent, this volume is a treasure trove of information. After establishing the importance of technology to "digital natives" (teens) who incorporate technology into virtually every facet of their lives, Braun goes on to explain the various technologies to "digital immigrants" (older generations). For those not knowledgeable about wikis, blogs, and podcasts, this book offers good definitions and insight into their applications. Want to know what a vodcast is? Or what folksonomy means? This volume explains new technologies in a user-friendly way. Most important, Braun gives concrete examples of how to integrate various forms of technology into adults' work with teenagers. Specific projects, such as teens writing wikis for the library and adding user comments to book descriptions in the library catalog, are highlighted and explained. Extremely helpful appendixes supply the teacher or librarian with sites to visit for solid information, further ideas, and examples.

Revelatory and sharp, this unique book offers a wonderful overview of the various technologies used by teens and supplies great material for educators as well. The many mind-expanding ideas offered by Braun are sure to guarantee positive interactions with teen students and library patrons.-Rachelle Bilz.

Braun, Linda W., Hillias J. Martin, and Connie Urquhart. **Risky Business: Taking and Managing Risks in Library Services for Teens**. American Library Association, 2010. 168p. $55. Trade pb. 978-0-8389-3596-5. Index. Source notes. Appendix. **VOYA** February 2011.

The authors participated in the "inspiring conversations of the 2009-2010 YALSA Presidential Task Force" and decided to write this book on the "risky business" of teen librarianship. The eight chapters and seven appendixes identify these risks, evaluate their necessity, and offer help in their implementation. In examining risk-worthy library collections, the book furnishes input from four "edgy" authors, including Ellen Hopkins. She states why books such as Tricks (teen prostitution) and Identical (incest) are important for teens. The Appendixes introduce the risk- taking librarians and include forms to assess "risk readiness," and to evaluate potential risky endeavors. Additional appendixes list forty developmental assets for adolescents, such as acquiring a positive identity, and also include more resources such as YALSA White Papers.

Thesis-style in appearance, this interesting book contains constructive information for teachers, parents, and, certainly, professional librarians. However, it also underscores the role that the general population has in being an advocate for teen library services. Reading books by Hopkins and others may dissuade teens from risky behavior or help them manage or extricate themselves from a troublesome situation. Throughout, theory is supported with examples, such as Ray Lusk's experimentation in implementing a Teen Summer Reading

Program (p.51-53).With Lusk and others, flops and successes are both learning tools. The chapter on technology is particularly vital in its discussion of on-line services such as book discussions and it offers practical advice in using social networking. This book will be a great resource for librarians and others who provide teen services.—Barbara Johnston.

Brehm-Heeger, Paula. **Serving Urban Teens**. Libraries Unlimited, 2008. 229p. $40 Trade pb. 978-1-59158-377-6. Index. Source Notes. Further Reading. Appendix. **VOYA** August 2008.

This book is a must-have for any librarian who works with youth. Written by an experienced practitioner and past-president of the Young Adult Library Services Association (YALSA), a division of the American Library Association (ALA), this thirteenth title in the Libraries Unlimited Professional Guides for Young Adult Librarians series begins with definitions and a brief history of library services to urban teens, followed by a description of issues concerning this special group. The remaining chapters detail every aspect of making positive connections with teens, from training staff-the entire library staff-to making space, developing the collection, designing programs, and developing partnerships within the community.

Using simple, direct language, Brehm-Heeger, who admits to being a library latch-key socializer in her younger years, gives practical advice. Her tables and checklists are in ready-to-go format. Youth librarians can take this book and run with it. Despite their sometimes erratic behavior, teens are important to the survival of libraries. It is not only the mission of libraries but also in their self-interest to capture the minds and hearts of youth while they can. This book provides the tools to accomplish the job.-Laura Woodruff.

Brenner, Miranda. **Understanding Manga and Anime**. Libraries Unlimited, 2007. 333p. $40 Trade pb. 978-1-59158-332-5. Glossary. Index. Illus. Biblio. Source Notes. Further Reading. Appendix. **VOYA** December 2007.

No question about it, Brenner's work is the definitive guide on this popular genre that has been a staple in Asia for generations and is now burning up the shelves in bookstores across the United States. Texts like **Graphic Novels in Your Media Center: A Definitive Guide** by Alison A. W. Lyga and Barry Lyga (Libraries Unlimited, 2004/**VOYA** April 2004) are like baby food compared to the steak in this guide. School media specialists and young adult librarians who have avoided adding manga or have approached building this portion of their collection with timidity because of ignorance or fear of censorship need tremble no more. Brenner provides thorough explanation of manga and anime vocabulary, potential censorship issues because of cultural disparities, and typical manga conventions. The author does not stop there but frequently includes illustrations from popular works to exemplify and highlight explanations. Even those librarians who consider themselves experts on the genre will be pleased to find tidbits of information that will make them more equipped to converse with hardcore fans. Hesitant Language Arts teachers would also benefit from exploring this tome to understand the value of manga for building vocabulary and reading skills.

Most impressive are the "Best OF" lists that complete every chapter. These lists contain not only publisher information and series plots and themes but also accurate age rating that can take hours to research online and that vendors often mislabel. Equally helpful are the appendixes with must-know vocabulary words and FAQs that highlight key points in the defense of manga—amazingly done in two pages. Frankly no professional collection could possibly be complete all-inclusive and exceptional work.—Erin Kilby.

Butler, Rebecca P. **Copyright for Teachers and Librarians in the 21st Century.** Neal-Schuman, 2011. 276p. $70. Oversize pb. 978-1-55570-738-5. Table of Contents. Bibliography. Appendices. Glossary. Index. **VOYA** December 2011.

Updating a standard reference book from 2004, the author draws from a series of workshops and classes to provide K-12 teachers, librarians, and other school employees with a handbook on copyright laws and fair-use guidelines. She describes through each chapter basic concepts like public domain, obtaining permission, documentation and licenses, open sourcing, plagiarism, and state laws, and provides updated information on new applications employing the use of the Internet, DVDs, CDs, video streaming, television, computer software, music and audio materials, and other multimedia. Public librarians will appreciate the chapter on interlibrary loans and the book's coverage of licensing agreements for electronic resources. The most helpful additions to this edition are the flowcharts throughout the book that take all the technical information and simplify them for easier understanding and decision making. Each chapter has a concluding paragraph which defines the highlights of that chapter. The index is thorough and accurate, particularly in providing easy access to the book's flowcharts. Almost all the references cited in each chapter's bibliography are for sources dated since 2009, and are mostly online resources.

As with the original text, this guide is a well thought-out guide to a complex topic. It is a much-needed, although unfortunately pricey, update that is highly recommended for all school and public libraries.—Kevin Beach.

Cantrell, Jan. **Students Harassing Students: The Emotional and Educational Toll on Kids.** Scarecrow Press, 2008. 144p. PLB $70. 978-1-57886-858-2. $24.95 Trade pb. 978-1-57886-861-2. Further Reading. **VOYA** April 2010.

Cantrell structures this book in such a way that it increases the reader's awareness of the problem of sexual harassment without lecturing. The scenarios that begin each chapter show how the problem is not merely an incident between students but is also fueled by the attitudes and lack of clarity on the part of the staff—from teachers to principals. Peer-to-peer sexual harassment is an age-old behavior that continues with the unconscious support of adults who do not see the seriousness of it. Grounded in experience, research, and school law, Cantrell sees the totality of this destructiveness, provides a clear process to deal with the problem, and reinforces the school's legal responsibilities. The author also points out that a sexual harassment policy will not solve the problem, but that without one, there is very little chance the environment will change.

This excellent resource should not be missed as it provides needed tools to create a healthier environment for both students and adults, whether staff or parents.—C. J. Bott.

Cart, Michael, and Christine A. Jenkins. **The Heart Has Its Reasons: Young Adult Literature with Gay/Lesbian/Queer Content, 1969-2004**. Scarecrow Press, 2006. 224p. PLB $46.20. 978-0-8108-5071-2. Index. Charts. Biblio. Chronology. Appendix. **VOYA** August 2006.

Writing a critical study of young adult novels having homosexual, or less commonly, bisexual or transgender themes seems almost an act of courage in our highly polarized society. Yet here is a definitive work on the subject. Using a chronological approach, the authors examine nearly two hundred books that have appeared since the 1969 publication of John Donovan's book, **I'll Get There, It Better Be Worth the Trip** (Harper & Row, 1969). Each chapter analyzes the most important books of a decade beginning with the 1970s, discusses plots and points of view, and concludes with a comprehensive annotated bibliography of titles. Following the 1990s is a chapter titled "A New Literature for a New Century?" This bibliographic essay considers the first four years of the twenty-first century and concludes with a year-by-year annotated bibliography. Finally the authors make a plea for more teenage fiction that deals honestly and realistically with issues of sexuality and shows true literary merit, providing multidimensional characters, verisimilitude, and an original voice.

Thoughtful and insightful analysis is a real strength of the book. The appendixes will also be useful, particularly the comparison between the development of African American literature for young people and that of books dealing with gay issues; and a chart of 191 novels arranged alphabetically by author and showing portrayals, content, and roles of gay protagonists, either primary or secondary. But here an explanation of abbreviations would be helpful. This book will be important for those wishing to make their library holdings more inclusive or who want to understand the changes that have occurred in this YA genre from the 1970s through the year 2004.-Rayna Patton.

Cavanaugh, Terence and Jerome Burg. **Bookmapping: Lit Trips and Beyond**. ISTE, 2011. 150p. $34.95 Oversize pb. 978-1-56484-283-1. **VOYA** June 2011.

It is often discussed in educational circles that students in the United States do not know their geography. In many cases, this is because too many courses are taught in a vacuum. Fiction is taught in language arts and/or reading classrooms, and geography is taught in social studies classrooms. Combining the two happens occasionally, but usually requires time-intensive planning. Bookmapping: Lit Trips provides ideas on how teachers can use elements from different disciplines in their own classrooms. The majority of authors and examples are from middle school, but there are high school-level course suggestions as well. Pairing a piece of literature and mapping seems to be a combination more suited to elementary school, but it works well at the upper levels because more advanced technology can be used. One chapter covers a high school computer science teacher who, through the use of reading about explorations, has his students create their own Google Earth bookmaps, with icons, layering, placemark banners, and photo overlays that are then shared with their classmates and the world by being published online. Other information includes using Google Earth, sources for images, Bing maps, information on creating your own bookmaps, instruction for bookmaps done individually and in cooperation with another teacher's class or classes, how to set up mapping in the classroom, and exploring existing bookmaps available on the Web. Most chapters include references, and there are sample lesson plans, and ISTE standards.

This book should be in the professional collection of every middle and high school library, preferably in every classroom.—Suanne B. Roush.

**Censored Books II: Critical Viewpoints, 1985-2000.** Nicholas J. Karolides, Ed. Scarecrow, 2002. 504p. PLB $55. 978-0-8108-4147-5. Index. Source Notes. **VOYA** October 2002.

Although new intellectual freedom issues have surfaced post-September 11, censorship still remains a critical area for librarians and educators. Like its predecessor, **Censored Books: Critical Viewpoints** (Scarecrow, 1993), which covered the years from 1950-1985, the purpose of this volume is to "provide rationales for teachers and other citizens in defense of frequently censored/challenged books." Nat Hentoff's foreword sets the stage with brief but vivid examples of censorship in action. Karolides's introduction includes an update on censorship, noting that an analysis provided by People for the American Way indicates that the scope of censorship is broadening beyond attacks on single books to entire programs and through legislative initiatives.

The heart of the book, however, is the sixty-four essays on books for children, teens, and adults that have been challenged frequently during that period covered in the book. Some of the books discussed are **Bridge to Teribithia, A Day No Pigs Would Die, The Giver, The House of the Spirits, Kaffir Boy, My Brother Sam is Dead**, and the *Harry Potter* series. Each essay is brief but packed with information and insights that show the value and worth of these books to readers and will help provide a foundation on which to build a defense of each book. This resource is readable on its own for any librarian, educator, or citizen with an interest in why books are so often viewed as dangerous and why the right to read must be protected.—Dolores Maminski.

**Change in Young Adult Literature** (HarperCollins, 1996).—Diane P. Tuccillo.

**Excellence in Library Services to Young Adults: The Nation's Top Programs.** 3rd Ed. Mary K. Chelton, Ed. Young Adult Library Services Association/American Library Association, 2000. 78p. Trade pb. 978-0-8389-0786-3. O.P. Index. **VOYA** December 2000.

Another stellar collection of thirty young adult library programs recognized by the Young Adult Library Services Association (YALSA) follows 1994 and 1998 editions (the second was selected for **VOYA**'s October 1998 *Five-Foot Bookshelf* as essential professional reading). Two- to four-page spreads contain descriptions, customers, community, setting and funding for both school and public library programs. The top five programs range from "Partners in Reading," in which eighth graders from South East Junior High School trade reading notebooks with adult volunteers in Iowa City, Iowa; to "Senior Sunday," in which the public library in Medford, Oregon, opens one Sunday exclusively to assist high school seniors with research projects. Other programs are arranged in eight subject categories such as collaborative efforts between libraries and community agencies, intergenerational programs, reading promotion, and youth participation. Highlights are a "Youth Stars" high school performing arts festival at Seattle Public Library that involves community groups and schools; a "Community Support for

Health Teens Forum" in response to the Columbine school shootings that brought teens, parent, educators, counselors, and citizens together in a panel discussion at Teton County Library in Jackson, Wyoming; and the "Lunch 'n' Lit" program for homeschoolers that meets in a King County public library in North Bend, Washington.

Though this **Excellence** volume needs no introduction for librarians who rely on it for inspiration, its introduction sets it apart from previous editions: editor Chelton puts her doctoral research in "Adult-Adolescent Service Encounters" into context for YA library services. It is library staff's hostile or suspicious attitudes toward "normal teen behavior and appearance," Chelton declares, "that create formidable barriers to good customer service." Her clear examples of adult versus teen perceptions and resulting misinterpretations give enormous insight into adult-teen relations. These superb programs illustrate how vital libraries can be when such relations work.—Catherine Dunn MacRae.

Crane, Beverly E. **Using Web 2.0 Tools in the K–12 Classroom**. Neal-Schuman, 2009. 189p. $59.95 Trade pb. 978-1-55570-653-1. Glossary. Index. Photos. Charts. Biblio. Further Reading. Appendix. **VOYA** June 2009.

Most teachers and librarians are well aware of the growing popularity of Web 2.0 technologies, but they might be hesitant to integrate blogs, wikis, podcasts, and the like into a structured classroom environment. This book provides step-by-step instructions on incorporating collaborative tools into existing curriculum by leveraging the best of today's social software. Crane suggests the outcome of such integration should not only develop expertise in the various technologies but also enhance other skills such as writing, grammar, problem solving, and critical thinking. Each chapter addresses a particular technology and describes what it is, how it works, and why it can be beneficial in a learning environment. A variety of subject disciplines across multiple grade levels (K–12) are depicted in real-world examples and include literature, social studies, science, and English as a second language. Screenshots and links to sites created by other educators empower the reader to visually and intellectually research the concept before actually implementing it. The book offers sample exercises, checklists, and progress reports to establish student goals and learning outcomes; a companion Web site provides additional exercises, tips on each tool, and periodic technology updates.

Crane's book is a "how-to" and "why should I?" manual all rolled into one easy-to-understand text. It is firmly grounded in traditional education strategies and methodologies, yet it provides insight into current academic and technology trends. This excellent resource should be widely appealing to teachers, librarians and school media specialists.—Judith Brink-Drescher.

Crews, Kenneth D. **Copyright Law for Librarians and Educators: Creative Strategies & Practical Solutions, 3rd Ed.** American Library Association, 2011. 208p. $57 Oversize pb. 978-0-8389-1092-4. Index. Photos. Source Notes. Further Reading. Appendixes. **VOYA** June 2012.

In this updated edition of a standard copyright resource for librarians, educators, and academics, copyright expert Crews has revised his text to ensure readers have a solid grounding in the latest developments in copyright law. Since the previous edition in 2006, courts have made new rulings on numerous copyright issues, including fair use and digital rights management, while at the same time, libraries have been ambitiously digitizing collections and creating myriad new websites for Internet users to access and peruse. Among other objectives, this book can help libraries ensure success in their efforts to create and promote online collections and resources by working within copyright law.

Crews presents information in a systematic manner, with key points outlined at the start of each chapter and scenarios for the reader to consider interspersed throughout the book. A quite readable text that can be studied cover to cover or used as a reference source as needed, this book, by the director of the Copyright Advisory Office at Columbia University and a teacher in their law school, belongs in every library.—Elaine Gass Hirsch.

Danner, Brandy. **A VOYA Guide to Apocalyptic, Post-Apocalyptic, and Dystopian Books and Media**. VOYA Press, 2012. 244p. $50. 978-1-61751-005-2.
   **A VOYA Guide to Apocalyptic, Post-Apocalyptic, and Dystopian Books and Media** was not reviewed in **VOYA**.

Davis, Stan, with Julia Davis. **Empowering Bystanders in Bullying Prevention**. Research Press, 2007. 218p. $29.95 Trade pb. with DVD. 978-0-87822-539-2. Biblio. Source Notes. Appendix. **VOYA** December 2007.
   Most schools confronting the problem of bullying tend to focus on the bully and the targeted student. But bystanders make up approximately eighty percent of the student population, and common sense says that involving those bystanders is crucial to the success of any bully-prevention program. Although this excellent professional resource reports on a prevention program in a K-6 building, it can change the thinking of the staff in all grades and reinforce citizen responsibility at all levels. Julia Davis explains in an appendix how she has used the same principles and techniques with teenagers. Among the many ideas and strategies in this book, two stand out. First, good bully prevention can have goals similar to the Neighborhood Watch program because such a program helps people be aware of their responsibility to others in the community. In addition, more cannot be asked of the students than of the staff. The authors clearly present the foundation of this program through a variety of lessons, discussions based upon open-ended questions, and many other activities, including magic tricks.
   After working this program for eight years, the authors found that students developed a stronger sense of justice, honesty, and fair treatment and a drive to value and help others instead of passively observing bullying behaviors or supporting bullies with silence. A bully prevention program aimed at the largest percentage of students makes sense. Although other programs have used this approach, none are as accessible or do it as well as this one.—C.J. Bott.

Dellasega, Cheryl, and Charisse Nixon. **Girl Wars: 12 Strategies That Will End Female Bullying**. Simon & Schuster, 2003. 243p. $14 Trade pb. 978-0-7432-4987-4. Appendix. **VOYA** December 2004.

It starts early and it goes on for a very long time. Girls bully each other with gossip, hallway whispers, notes on lockers and desktops, and the obvious exclusion for any number of bizarre illogical reasons. Dellasego and Nixon talk about Relational Aggression (RA) in straightforward language-no jargon here. Because the indirect bullying is so difficult to witness, adults need to learn what to look for, and they need to listen. Eye rolling, hair flipping, whispers behind hands, notes passed around someone, empty seats beside the same girl everyday, students desperately trying to be invisible in the hallway, or eating in the staircase to avoid the lunchroom are all things of which to be aware. Anonymous aggression is particularly frightening. When a girl does not know who is targeting her, the whole world becomes enemy territory. Cyberbullying or Cyber-RA is on the rise. Most young people are more computer savvy than the adults around them, and that know-how plus the harassment makes the targeted girl feel powerless and isolated.

This book is written for adults to help them understand and prevent RA. Adults of both genders need to read it and understand how deeply RA hurts. Help is here. This book is a professional must-read for anyone working with girls from the early grades on up.-C. J. Bott.

**Developing an Information Literacy Program K-12: A How-to-Do-It Manual and CD-ROM Package**, 2nd Ed. Developed by the Iowa City Community School District. Mary Jo Langhorne, Ed. Neal-Schuman, 2004. 432p. $89.95 Trade pb. 978-1-55570-509-1. Index. Illus. Biblio. **VOYA** August 2005.

The first edition of this book (1998/ **VOYA August** 1999) is a treasure, but this expanded revision is equally valuable. The objective of the information literacy curriculum of the authoring school district is collaboration between media specialists and classroom teachers. It is the practical manual for instituting the practices that the American Association of School Librarians (AASL), a division of the American Library Association (ALA), advocates through Information Power (ALA, 1998/ **VOYA August** 1999). This second edition is organized by the five-step process that the district uses for research. Within that information literacy model, the librarian has the opportunity to teach everything from use of the library catalog and other electronic databases to selecting a good book to read for pleasure. Lessons are now included about accessing and assessing Internet sites. A major challenge for a teacher of research skills is imparting the ability to evaluate resources. Although it used to be the purview of college professors to train students to question their resources, typically books and periodicals, now teachers in middle school must lead students to question how they know a given Web site is reliable. The district has added lessons on note taking; extracting information without plagiarizing is an essential skill. There is even a nod to independent reading for pleasure because a good reader is more likely to be a successful researcher. A helpful organizational feature is the addition of text boxes that say exactly which information literacy standards are being taught and at what level, as well as other text boxes that keep track of exactly where the user is in the five steps, keeping clear what grade level is accomplishing which skill with a given lesson.

But what if your district uses The Big Six? Or the elaborate twelve? Or twenty-five steps to perfect papers? What if they do Iowa and you do Ohio? Although it is specific for the curriculum and resources used by the Iowa City Community School District, this book and its accompanying Microsoft-based CD are easily adapted to the needs of any teacher and student doing research. The diagrams, lessons, and presentations are there, digitally ready to be modified to fit individual needs. Use their framework and fill in a specific curriculum, or tug and pull at the framework itself until it does what is needed. The manual will be dog-eared, and the CD will make its home in or near the computer. The superb organization and content of both make them infinitely useful.-Lynne Hawkins.

Dewitt, Peter. **Dignity for All: Safeguarding LGBT Students**. Corwin, 2012. 136p. $25.95 Oversize pb. 978-1-4522-0590-8. **VOYA** August 2012.

The aim of this book is to encourage educators, including counselors, teachers, and administrators, to evaluate and gain insight into the current conditions in their classrooms in order to help LGBT students feel safer in the school environment. Recent statistics show close to 90 percent of these children have experienced harassment, up to and including verbal and physical, abuse within the walls of the school. Chapters on gay stereotypes, bullying, parental involvement, curriculum ideas, and the formation of alliance groups make this book a valuable resource guide for schools considering a course of action. The final chapters on following through, dealing with resistance, and reviewing recent success stories round out this constructive manual.

The themes of altering school policies and codes of conduct, along with securing the cooperation of staff, parents, and students, have helped make schools more positive and much safer places for victims of bullying and the associated verbal and physical torment. The National Association of School Psychologists worked in conjunction with the author to produce this guide. The template for the creation of a conduct code, the bibliography of additional articles and resources on LGBT school programs, and the useful index add to the value of this well-organized, compassionate volume. This is recommended for all high schools seeking progressive changes.—Kevin Beach.

Donham, Jean. **Enhancing Teaching and Learning: A Leadership Guide for School Library Media Specialists**. Neal-Schuman, 1998. 274p. $45 Trade pb. 978-1-55570-328-8. Index Charts. Biblio. Further Reading. **VOYA** December 1999.

School library media specialists will find theory, rationale, and implications perfectly balanced here with practical applications, practices, and policies. The chapter on assessing student work, for example, presents the definition, rationale, and construction of rubrics accompanied by a rubric for assessing rubrics. (*For readers outside the education field, rubrics are educational tools used to assess lessons. They assign value to assignments using difficulty and thoroughness as criteria for grading. For example, a one-page book report without pictures may be worth seventy points while a three-page report with graphics and an oral presentation could be worth one hundred points.*) There are also rubrics for note-taking and for writing thesis statements. Examples and templates are readily adoptable and/or adaptable, including: a sample monthly statistics report to administration; a parent survey; CD-ROM, video, and website evaluation forms; a pathfinder template; and rubrics for program evaluation.

The book is divided into two parts: the environment and the library media program. There are descriptions of roles, key characteristics of work situations with students, and curriculum and instruction. Also discussed are professional relationships with the principal, the school district, and the community, with implications for the leadership responsibilities of the school library media specialist. Collaborative planning, scheduling, collection development and maintenance, literacy, technology, and assessment of student work and the library media programs are the focus of the rest of the book. Each chapter culminates in a set of "action strategies" that provide specifically targeted tasks. Donham is articulate, clear, well-organized, and write fluently. Key points are supported and there is plenty of quotable material appropriate for sharing with colleagues. Definitive while not exhaustive, comprehensive yet concise, this resource would be my pick for the single most valuable professional text for school library media specialists.—Kim Carter.

Donham, Jean. **Enhancing Teaching and Learning: A Leadership Guide for School Library Media Specialists**, 2nd Ed. Neal-Schuman, 2005. 338p. Trade pb. 978-1-55570-516-9. O.P. Index. Source Notes. Further Reading. Appendix. **VOYA** August 2005.

Updated with the latest statistics and research, this resource exemplifies making the best better still. As Donham states in the preface, this new edition "is expanded to reflect changes-professional, theoretical, legal, and political-in the library media field and in education over the last six years." Statistics on current trends relating to the new generation of students highlight increased attention to secondary students, media, and reading habits. Learning theory research incorporates learning styles and motivation as educational roles, relationships, and collaboration are explored in more depth. Current issues of equity and standards are addressed, as is the impact of No Child Left Behind and technological developments. Leadership opportunities for school library media specialists in the changing educational environment are integrated throughout the book. A new chapter, "Leadership," reviews literature related to the "unique role of the library media specialist who leads from the middle." Each chapter ends with suggested action strategies related to the American Association of School Libraries (AASL) and the Association for Educational Communications Technology (AECT) Guidelines for Library Media Programs' three elements of the library media program: learning and teaching, information access and delivery, and program administration.

"Having influence requires establishing one's expertise, working collegially with others, articulating one's ideas clearly, maintaining a good 'say-do' ratio, . . . and establishing processes for continuous reflection and assessment." Donham succinctly provides a rich repertoire of tools for accomplishing all of the above. Worth the purchase price even if one already owns the first edition and a must-buy if one does not, this book remains this reviewer's personal "single most valuable professional text for school library media specialists." (A review of the first edition appears in **VOYA** December 1999.)-Kim Carter.

Donham, Jean. **Enhancing Teaching and Learning: A Leadership Guide for Library School Media Specialists**. 2nd Ed. Revised. Neal-Schman, 2008. 353p. $65 Trade pb. 978-1-55570-647-0. Index. Charts. Biblio. Further Reading. **VOYA** August 2009.

Originally published in 1998, this revised, updated edition incorporates the new Standards for the 21st Century Learner from the American Association of School Librarians (AASL). Donham comprehensively covers how to best implement a successful library media program in this thorough examination of the many facets in library media and education. Divided into two parts, this title first offers an in-depth look at The Environment, which focuses on the key relationships between the school media center and its stakeholders—the students, the principal, the community, and others—and how these relationships can result in a successful media program and thus a more effective learning environment. The second section, The Library Media Program, addresses topics ranging from collaborative planning and media center collections to program evaluation and leadership. Each chapter ends with action strategies, which are creative, practical applications of the concepts discussed, and a scenario for discussion, which offers thought-provoking situations of the principles considered. Donham also includes a select bibliography at the end of the book for supplemental reading.

This title is well-written, well-researched, and informative. Donham masterfully weaves together current AASL standards and the real world of today's media specialist. Media specialists and graduate students who are planning to become media specialists will find this resource to be invaluable.—Domina Daughtrey.

Doucett, Elisabeth. **Creating Your Library Brand**. ALA Editions, 2008. 124p. $50 Trade pb. 978-0-8389-0962-1. Glossary. Index. Appendix. **VOYA** December 2008.

The buzz in marketing right now is branding, but many libraries are put off from starting branding projects because they do not know how, consider it too large a project, or do not have extra funds. This book will help. Doucett's approach to branding takes each step as a single project, making it accessible and achievable. She defines marketing and branding and then offers practical advice on the different aspects, from creating a logo to using templates, working with outside help, and creating and evaluating the branding plan. She emphasizes including staff, patrons, and board members in the process and offers helpful examples with which one can follow up online. Doucett even provides a practical list of pitfalls in which she sees libraries get bogged down.

By breaking the chapters into individual steps for branding, Doucett makes this book a helpful guide for the beginner as well as the seasoned marketer. Each chapter stands on its own, so one can read or review whichever sections are needed. Doucett sprinkles her text with tips and FAQ boxes, plus exercises at the end of each section to provide a starting point for the project. Possibly even more helpful is the glossary of terms that marketers use regularly but with which beginners may not be familiar. This type of guide can serve as a useful ready reference, but be forewarned-marking helpful pages will require a book full of tabs.-Joyce Doyle.

Doyle, Miranda. **101+ Great Ideas for Teen Library Web Sites**. Neal-Schuman, 2007. 307p. $65 Trade pb. 978-1-55570-593-0. Index. Photos. Further Reading. **VOYA** December 2007.

A library's "face" on the Web is important, especially to today's teens who are used to finding information first on the Internet. With the tips in this book, libraries can use their Web sites more efficiently and reach teens in new, interactive ways, including IM, blogging, text messaging, and discussion boards. This book is divided into six major headings: Essential Web Site Know-How, which covers Web design and technology literacy; Communication, including publicizing, terms of usage, and user access to online interactive materials; Information, including online learning and reader's advisory; Tech Companion Pages, which starts with a useful glossary of online and technology terms; and Help Pages, with its bibliography of journal articles and books to assist librarians in making decisions about adding original and interactive content to their Web pages.

Any library with a Web site can benefit from the information in this book, which includes screencaps from successful teen library Web sites. Each design and technology tip is clearly explained and easy to understand, even for Web designers with minimal experience. In addition to receiving tips on reaching teens, readers are advised on ways to use their Web sites to achieve better school/library cooperation, including working to teach students how to avoid plagiarism and teaching test-taking practices. Part of the *Teens @ the Library* series, this book is the one to check out when considering a redesign of the library's Web site or looking for ideas on improving the site's usage.-Carlisle K. Webber.

**Empowering Learners: Guidelines for School Library Media Programs**. American Association of School Librarians, Eds. ALA Editions, 2009. 64p. $39 Trade pb. 978-0-8389-8519-9. Index. Biblio. Further Reading. **VOYA** December 2009.

New technologies for information and learning have necessitated changing basic guidelines for school library media programs over the years. Based on the American Association of School Librarians' *Standards for the 21st-Century Learner,* this resource presents the latest guidelines and standards for school libraries. Clearly written and cogently presented, this book begins with the 2009 revised mission statement of the school library media program (SLMP) and then delineates twenty-first-century skills, learners, and learning environments. Subsequent chapters tackle the myriad facets of the SLMP, from the roles of educators to learning environments and the collection. Following each guideline is a list of specific actions suggested for the school library media specialist (SLMS). Helpful sidebars such as "Factors to Consider When Building the Virtual Collection" and "Examples of Alternative Funding Sources" enrich the information in each chapter. The "Delve Deeper" lists found on almost every page refer the reader to a plethora of excellent resources, both print and online. Ten pages of appendixes contain helpful information such as the Library Bill of Rights.

Indispensable for any media specialist, this AASL resource provides both a blueprint for SLMP excellence and a valuable tool to highlight the importance of the SLMS as an integral part of the educational team. It makes essential additions and revisions to SLMP standards for twenty-first-century learners, thus arming the SLMS with information essential to maintaining the highest standards of service to school patrons.—Rachelle Bilz.

**Ethics in School Librarianship: A Reader**. Carol Simpson, Ed. Linworth, 2003. 120p. $44.95 Trade pb. 978-1-58683-084-7. Source Notes. Appendix. **VOYA** October 2004.

An "ethical framework" for school library media specialists is constructed through the different chapters by experts in the field, usefully bringing together in one volume discussions of professional ethics that apply to a large range of issues. These include collection development, access, confidentiality, use of technology, intellectual freedom, intellectual property, administration, and Internet use. As Simpson writes, "Reading about ethics is no walk in the park. The issues are thorny, and they can cause discomfort." Some of the thornier topics discussed include biases in the process of selecting materials, the consideration of whether the implementation of computer-based reading programs can violate ethics of access, the consideration of penalties for misuse of Internet access, and ways in which confidentiality can be breached in school library media centers. Of special interest are discussions on the differences between codes of ethics as practiced by teachers and the code of ethics advocated for library professionals, and the implications of codes of ethics for working relationships in the field. Suggestions and guidelines are provided to help the school library media specialist to think through and implement ethical codes.

The comprehensive approach and the provision of thought-provoking discussion questions for each chapter make this tool valuable for use in school library media education programs. The issues covered, however, are essential reading for all who work in the field of school librarianship. The ethical codes of the American Library Association and the Association of Communications and Technology are provided in an appendix.-Hilary Crew.

**Excellence in Library Services to Young Adults**, 4th Ed. Renée Vaillancourt Mc-Grath, Ed. ALA Editions, 2004. 80p. $20 Trade pb. 978-0-8389-8280-8. **VOYA** December 2004.

Twenty-five library programs for young adults are presented here to "inspire readers to create new and better young adult programs." Each was chosen through a Young Adult Library Services Association (YALSA) grant application process, judging entries on the degree to which the program meets the needs of the community; originality; how it reflects the concepts in New Directions for Library Service to Young Adults

(ALA, 2002/ **VOYA** October 2002); the degree to which it improves service to young adults; and the quality of the programs. The programs are organized into nine categories: After-School Programs, Career Preparation, Creative Expression, Life Skills, Literary Appreciation, Miscellany, Summer Reading, Teen Advisory Boards, and Young Adults with Disabilities. Basic information for each program is given, including program description, community demographics, how youth helped in the planning process, budget, evaluation, effect of the program on young adults, and contact information. Some programs are small budget. Poetry Alive!, a one-day poetry reading program at Pleasant Valley High School in Chico, California, is run for less than $50. Teen Productions, a series of three-day workshops as an alternative to a summer reading program at the Flint Public Library in Flint, Michigan, and Job Shadow Day in the University Heights Public Library in Cleveland Heights, Ohio, where students learn about being a librarian, were funded for less than $1,000. Other programs were funded by grants of several thousand dollars: Love and Sex: Making Choices at the Flint Public Library brought in an author to lead discussions on teen pregnancy in conjunction with the photography exhibit "Children of Children." Wired for Youth provides computer access and literary experiences for low-income students at the Austin Public Library in Austin, Texas. Many others count on partnerships with other community agencies for success, such as TIGERS, a program at the Franklin County Public Library in Eastpoint, Florida, that works to break negative cycles for youth by helping them reach individualized goals through success-oriented projects.

These programs are not packaged and ready to replicate, but they serve as an inspiration for creating innovative programming that fits individual communities. Readers are encouraged to modify the ideas to fit their own situations. This revised resource follows earlier versions edited by Mary K. Chelton (ALA Editions, 2000, 1997, 1994/ **VOYA** February 1998 and December 2000), and is a must-read for anyone doing young adult programming.-Deborah L. Dubois.

Feinstein, Sheryl G. **Secrets of the Teenage Brain: Research-Based Strategies for Reaching and Teaching Today's Adolescents, 2nd Ed**. Corwin Press, 2009. 202p. $32.95 Trade pb. 978-1-4129-6267-4. Glossary. Index. Illus. Photos. Biblio. **VOYA** April 2010.

If men are from Mars and women are from Venus, then from which planet do teenagers hail? Although every adult was once an adolescent, the brooding, unpredictable, and sometimes nightmarish behavior of young adults often keeps parents at their wit's end. The same can be said for those who have chosen to enlighten this teenaged group. The challenge in educating today's teenagers—beyond simply keeping them awake and motivated—is in having to grapple with more disturbing obstacles such as self-inflicting and destructive behaviors (e.g. anorexia, obesity, cutting), substance abuse, and violent, sometimes physical acts of outright aggression. This revised edition presents practical explanations as to why teenagers are literally wired the way they are by extensively examining how the brain functions during these transitional years. Gender differences are candidly discussed to offer helpful insight into demystifying many teen behaviors; typical misconceptions are identified and debunked in Secrets Revealed sections. For the classroom, bullet-point lists of "Instructional Strategies" and "Things to Try" are designed to help engage and motivate the adolescent learner.

The back of the book contains a summary of each chapter, book club discussion questions, a glossary of brain terms, and an extensive bibliography. Parents, teachers, and librarians should all benefit from this intelligently assembled and highly recommended resource.—Judith Brink-Drescher.

Ferlazzo, Larry. **English Language Learners: Teaching Strategies That Work**. Linworth, 2010. 184p. $35. 978-1-58683-524-8. Charts. Appendix. **VOYA** August 2010.

**English Language Learners: Teaching Strategies That Work** is a well-written, easy-to-understand handbook for all educators. It has all the elements educators look for in a resource book: readability, research-supported ideas, day-to-day activities that can be implemented immediately, plus an appendix full of resources. Ferlazzo uses five principals for teaching, not only for ELL students, but all students. The five principals are building strong relationships, accessing prior knowledge, identifying and mentoring leadership, learning by doing, and reflection. Each chapter thoroughly discusses one of the five principals, giving real life scenarios, activities, research, and technology ideas. Ferlazzo backs up his ideas with data from important researchers in education, such as Wormelli, Marzanno, and others. This book is a valuable resource for all educators, but especially teachers of English language learners, as well as struggling native English-speaking readers. In the fast-paced, high-stakes testing, merit-pay world in which educators currently find themselves, it is exciting to find well-researched books with easy-to-implement ideas that help to improve student learning. This will be a great addition to any educator's library.—Lana Trulove.

Foster, James C. **BONG HiTS 4 JESUS: A Perfect Constitutional Storm in Alaska's Capital**. University of Alaska Press, 2010. 373p. $29.95 pb. 978-1-60223-089-7. Notes. Bibliography. Index. Chronology. **VOYA** "The First Freedom" October 2011.

In **BONG HiTS 4 JESUS: A Perfect Constitutional Storm in Alaska's** Capital, political scientist James C. Foster presents an authoritative case study enhanced by personal interviews with twenty-seven players in the drama. A teacher of American constitutional law at Oregon State University, Foster skillfully weighs the case's significance. The escalation of this incident into "almost seven years of increasingly acrimonious disputing," he says, reflects the dogmatism of twenty-first-century American policy. With a slogan ironically combining bong with Jesus, misfit prankster Frederick defends "his own rights" as "the hero of student expression," says Foster, while misunderstood principal Morse asserts "her own virtuousness" as "the protector of student safety." Foster asks: Was the Glacier Avenue incident "dangerous drug speech or sophomoric student stunt?"

Attorney Mertz filed suit for injury against Morse and the school district. Morse's attorney, David Crosby, claimed school immunity. Their divergent narratives hardly seemed to describe the same occurrence. As the case moved through courts that reversed each decision, Mertz and Crosby became infuriated with each other. The case also polarized Juneau itself, isolated on a mountainous coastline. These opposing sides reveal constitutional law's "abiding tension" between "individual rights and social order," says Foster.

Foster's meticulous account of the Morse v. Frederick Supreme Court proceedings—with well-known Kenneth Starr representing Morse, and Mertz continuing with Frederick—has "you are there" suspense. Scrutinizing the split Morse decision plus its five separate opinions from justices with varying interpretations, Foster describes the case's outcome as "no less ambiguous than Frederick's banner."

The majority summary by Chief Justice John G. Roberts Jr. holds that "a principal can restrict students' speech at a school event when that speech is reasonably viewed as promoting illegal drug use." The dissent by Justices Stevens, Souter, and Ginsburg finds Frederick's message "obscure nonsense" and his explanation that he just wanted to get on television credible; they note that "most students . . . do not shed their brains at the schoolhouse gate."

"Morse is a mess," concludes Foster. This "incoherent" ruling "fails to guide Americans how to proceed when grappling with reconciling student speech with school discipline in the context of adolescent drug use." Legal wranglings continued for seventeen months.

The November 2008 settlement specified that the school would hold a forum about student free speech rights—as did the failed 2002 mediation. Frederick maintained that his banner did not advocate drug use. The School Board maintained that Morse's interpretation of the banner was reasonable. "They had devoted six and a half years to getting back to where they started," says Foster.

In 2009, at age twenty-five, Frederick confessed to Foster that he regretted not dropping the case. He wishes students still had those drug speech rights that the Supreme Court's Morse decision limited. Unfortunately, this message about unintended consequences is relegated to an endnote.

The First Amendment contains a compelling alternative to legal disputes. Its speech clause's "core value," Foster points out, is "conversing." He reimagines Glacier Avenue with the alternate conversation that Morse should have led, engaging Frederick respectfully and suggesting they go inside to discuss "rights and responsibilities." Offering options such as holding a mock Supreme Court or community dialogue, Foster challenges us to create civility.

In Juneau last summer, finding the spot on Glacier Avenue where Frederick held his banner, I established beyond my reasonable doubt that he was not on school property. A Juneau resident, still stinging from the controversy that tore his town apart, showed me a treasured possession: teacher Clay Good's original photograph of the banner. It's on the cover of this groundbreaking citizens' guide.—Cathi Dunn MacRae

Fuhrken, Charles. **What Every Elementary Teacher Needs to Know About Reading Tests: (From Someone Who Has Written Them)**. Stenhouse Publishers, 2011. 244p. $24. Oversize pb. 978-1-57110-885-2. Index. Charts. Appendices. **VOYA** June 2012.

In this teacher resource book, Charles Fuhrken, a test developer who has helped write assessment tests for several states, offers his inside knowledge about the structure of middle school reading assessment tests and strategies to help students and teachers prepare for them. Four main sections cover basic test lexicon; commonly assessed reading standards (such as vocabulary development and literary techniques); sample passages and test items with tips alongside; and a compilation of resources and reading activities to use in the classroom. Appendices provide charts and reproducibles for these activities.

Fuhrken writes in a clear, straightforward manner, much like the test items he develops. By providing examples and references when discussing the field of education, he makes his work accessible to educators with varying degrees of experience. Though teachers may criticize such an overt "teaching to the test" approach, Fuhrken acknowledges that, regardless of one's stance on the efficacy of assessment tests, they are pervasive in today's schools, and knowledge is power for teachers and students alike. His peeks behind the curtain of test item construction serve to enlighten and empower both groups; as he states, "Confidence comes as a result of a deep awareness of test formats, test language, test tasks, test logic, and other test features..." Teacher guidance will be required for middle school students to find this book's information palatable and useful; middle school libraries with professional collections and public libraries with parent/teacher collections will want to make sure to purchase it.—Rebecca O'Neil.

Gorman, Michele. **Getting Graphic! Using Graphic Novels to Promote Literacy with Preteens and Teens**. Linworth, 2003. 140p. $36.95 Trade pb. 978-1-58683-089-2. Glossary. Index. Illus. Charts. Biblio. Source Notes. Appendix. **VOYA** June 2004.

Aiming to provide a solid introduction to a format that might still be unfamiliar to school librarians and others working with young adults and books, Austin Public Library's Wired for Youth librarian succeeds in delivering guidance that is immediately useful. Following a brief overview of comics in American popular culture and a quick survey of readily reproducible programs using graphic novels to promote reading, the bulk of the book is a series of annotated recommendations sorted by appropriate target audience. Of particular note is the concise and inspired table of "Graphic Novels and Literary Devices," which spells out specific ways in which titles address curricular demands. Appendixes address such concerns as designing collection development and reconsideration policies that support graphic novel collections.

The annotations themselves, which cover nearly eighty different stand-alone works and several long-running series, do not always include specifics about possibly controversial details, but several types of coding (attached to grade level or denoting mature content) remind the librarian or teacher using this guide to look at the material for themselves before placing it in a local collection where it might not be suitable. Part of a growing body of professional attention to the format, Gorman's book is an excellent tool for both collection developers and those wondering how to connect potential young readers to the graphic novel collection that they are building.-Francisca Goldsmith.

Graham, Warren. **Black Belt Librarian: Real World Safety & Security**. American Library Association, 2011. 104p. $45 Oversize pb. 978-0-8389-1137-2. **VOYA** April 2012.

As Graham states, "No library wants problem patrons, but they are coming." As librarians, we know that even as our staff size has shrunk in the last few years, our patron base has increased. With this increase in use, many branches have noticed an increase in the number of patrons who may pose a security threat. Bringing over twenty-five years of experience as a security officer and manager for the public library of Charlotte, Graham helps librarians reflect on their security procedures and whether current procedures are adequately safeguarding staff members and patrons. Graham sets out a straightforward twelve-step program that will help improve the security of any library, regardless of the size or type of population served. The steps include the importance of consistently enforcing all rules, using simple documentation, maintaining a security checklist, and establishing regular trainings for staff. These steps seem simple but are often overlooked by management and staff.

This short guide packs a great deal of tips into nine succinct chapters. "Stories from the trenches" will make some readers laugh and others cringe; however, what this book does best is require the reader to reflect on their own behaviors and to examine their confidence level when working with problem patrons. After all, a librarian's reaction to an incident can help escalate or deescalate a situation very quickly. A chapter on day-to-day security considerations, creating basic security documentation, and hiring the best security personnel will provide managers with tools for gearing up security protocol. This guide would be a meaningful addition to any public or academic library professional bookshelf.—Amy Wyckoff.

Grover, Robert J. and Fowler, Susan G. **Helping Those Experiencing Loss: A Guide to Grieving Resources**. Libraries Unlimited, 2011. $50. Oversize pb. 234p. 978-1-59884-826-7. Index. Appendix.**VOYA** December 2011.

Husband and wife authors, Grover and Fowler, use their considerable librarianship credentials to compile this invaluable resource of grief literature that is designed to help professionals (in the education, library, and mental health fields), as well as parents, work with people of all ages to face the myriad issues surrounding deep loss. The authors detail the developmental stages of grief for young adults and cover a wide range of losses. In addition to death (of parents, relatives, friends, teachers, pets), children may suffer emotional fallout from divorce, from learning that they are adopted, or from being put into the foster care system. Grover and Fowler also spend some time discussing the challenges of parents who are experiencing their own enormous loss (spouse, child, parent) and yet must continue to care for their children.

The uniform organization of each chapter provides easy access to the relevant information for each topic. A chapter overview is followed by lengthy essays on the targeted issues, citing research findings, and current theories. They are divided by topic and include ordering information and lengthy annotations. The bibliographies for the children's and young adults' chapters also specify age range. The hefty price tag, while a concern for strapped and shrinking budgets, is worth the investment. Working with stricken children is especially wrenching and this wonderful resource offers not only the comfort of a guided plan, but also provides reassuring explanations for all the emotional triggers, supported by appropriate readings.—Beth Andersen.

Harris, Frances Jacobson. **I Found It on the Internet: Coming-of-Age Online**. ALA Editions, 2005. 160p. $35 Trade pb. 978-0-8389-0898-3. Index. Illus. Biblio. **VOYA** August 2005.

Unlike many other library and information studies professional authors, Harris understands that for teenagers, technology is where information and communication meet with consequences, both good and bad and often unintended, for both the teens and the library. She points out that most youth information-seeking research has studied formal information systems for schoolwork but has little examined teenagers' use of informal systems and the way in which communication technologies bridge the gap between them for teenagers. Libraries prohibit or seriously ration their use without taking this merged bridging function into account, deeming such uses frivolous. Instead Harris coins the acronym "ICTs" for merged information and communication technologies, calling these "social information spaces" or "environments in which people use communication technology to access information, manipulate it, transform it, and exchange it." She then proceeds to discuss the ones that have the most influence on teenage life, taking each in turn and giving examples of how teenagers use them. Examples include blogs and online diaries, e-mail, instant messaging, usenet and message boards, electronic discussion lists, chat rooms, peer-to-peer file sharing, Web-based homework help sites, and interactive "Ask an Expert" services. Among the consequences discussed are the decline of civil discourse, identity formation and self-expression, a feeling of independence, keeping parents at bay, getting there without going anywhere, joining a community and socializing, inadvertent loss of privacy and conflict, collaboration and gaming, cheating, plagiarism, hacking, harassment and bullying, and access to inappropriate content, among others. Harris concludes with a teaching and learning agenda to help youth behave well online and be able to evaluate what they find, and discusses how traditional library service might adapt to the existence of this new environment in adolescents' lives.

Harris provides by far the best book on technology and adolescents that this reviewer has read to date. It is well-grounded in research (including my own), good practice, and an innate but highly informed understanding of adolescent development.-Mary K. Chelton.

Heins, Marjorie. **Not in Front of the Children: "Indecency," Censorship, and the Innocence of Youth**. Hill and Wang, 2001. 402p. $23.95 Trade pb. 978-0-8135-4221-8. **VOYA,** *The View from VOYA*, August 2002.

>**Not in Front of the Children: "Indecency," Censorship, and the Innocence of Youth** is a seminal work at the heart of youth advocacy. Its title reveals that Heins places youth at front row center in the censorship debate. In this encompassing analysis of all types of censorship, never once does Heins's focus waver from its effect on youth. Most censorship attempts stems from society's concern for protecting youth, yet Heins asserts that it is our desire to prevent harm to minors that damages them.

>A First amendment lawyer who directs the Free Expression Project of the National Coalition Against Censorship, Heins devotes half of her exhaustive study to a historical overview of the evolution of protectionism. Citing landmark publications and cases in the context of their times, Heins tracks the development of questions that still plague us. How can minors be censored separately from adults? Why are the censorship decisions so often based on adults' withholding of societal approval of sexual or violent content—even if materials are not proven to cause promiscuity or delinquent behavior? And the most basic question of all: do minors have First Amendment rights?

>Beyond the book and school journalism cases familiar to librarians and educators, Heins also explores broadcast censorship, sexuality education, and Internet filtering. Her analysis of media effects research casts doubt on the much-touted harmful effects of TV and movie violence on young viewers. Inexact social science research techniques try to "quantify aesthetic experience, . . . looking for simplistic explanations of extremely complex phenomena."

>Heins calls for a "no-censorship policy even for youth," not "such an alarming prospect" once readers absorb her arguments against "harm-to-minors rhetoric" and "intellectual protectionism." Her final chapter is an eloquent plea for youth advocacy through "affirmative approaches" such as media literacy programs, "finely calibrated judgments" of minors' First Amendment rights with "age- and maturity-based distinctions," and understanding of the nature of youth. Defenders of youth's intellectual freedom cannot afford not to digest Heins's inspiring and rigorous resource.--Catherine Dunn MacRae.

Herald, Diana Tixier, and Bonnie Kunzel. **Strictly Science Fiction**. Libraries Unlimited, 2002. 300p. PLB $55. 978-1-56308-893-3. Index. Biblio. Further Reading. Appendix. **VOYA** December 2002.

>Although these two competing readers' advisory works cover just about the same ground, the differences in treatment grant them unique strengths. Buker's work is well-organized but slightly idiosyncratic, resembling nothing so much as a long, fruitful chat with a buddy who really knows his science fiction. Aimed at those poor folks on the reference desk, who panic and freeze when asked to recommend a good SF or fantasy title, it is both easy to use and guaranteed to produce results. Divided into two major sections, one for science fiction and one for fantasy, the thirty-three chapters cover everything from works on alien contact and killer computers to "Talking Cats, Dragons, Elves, and Other Mythological Beasties." Each chapter begins with a short essay, outlining the history and major trends in the facet of the genre being treated, followed

by selected annotated titles, a list of other recommended titles, and "Derek's Pick." In some instances, a "Best Pick for the Reluctant Reader" is also included. Whatever their patrons' tastes in either of these two speculative genres, librarians will find recommended books listed with witty annotations-Buker is sort of a librarian's Anthony Lane. The book ends with lists of award-winning books and a comprehensive, accurate index.

Herald and Kunzel's work treats, as stated in the title, science fiction only-although Herald's earlier excellent **Fluent in Fantasy** (Libraries Unlimited, 2000/ **VOYA** December 1999), fills that gap admirably. A more scholarly treatment than Buker's above, the Herald and Kunzel book is divided into eight categories, treating action-adventures, technology, the future of Earth, alien contact, cross-genre titles, books for young readers, short stories, and a list of resources for librarians. Each chapter begins with a few paragraphs on the particular aspect of science fiction being treated, moving to an annotated list of books arranged alphabetically by author. Icons by the annotations note whether the book is particularly suited to teens, is an award winner, or has been made into a movie. The format and layout are particularly nice, with good use of white space and clear type. Chapters are tabbed for easy location, and the book concludes with appendixes listing award winners, best authors, and best books, as well as author/title, character, and subject indexes.

For most reference librarians, **Strictly Science Fiction** is a slightly better choice, due to the exemplary organization and layout-and the fact that the book lies open nicely. It would be a shame, however, to miss out on Buker's observations and tart comments. A really savvy reference librarian would want both.-Ann Welton.

Herald, Diana Tixier. **Teen Genreflecting: A Guide to Reading Interests**, 2nd Ed. Libraries Unlimited, 2003. 275p. PLB $45. 978-1-56308-996-1. Index. Further Reading. Appendix. **VOYA** June 2004.

Written for both expert and amateur young adult librarians, this clearly organized, easy-to-follow guide to literature for both middle and high school students makes it easy to answer the popular "I'm looking for a book on . . ." question. By using this resource, any readers' advisor can help a teen find an enjoyable and well-written book. The first chapter offers an overview of teen readers' advisory services, and subsequent chapters focus on popular genres of young adult literature, including but not limited to suspense, adventure, fantasy, alternate formats (including graphic novels), and Christian fiction. Both recent and classic YA books are listed in their appropriate genres, and every entry contains the author, title, publication date, and age level of the book in the style of **VOYA** 's codes. When appropriate, awards and any best lists on which a book might have appeared are cited. One especially helpful marking is the icon indicating that a book has been made into a movie.

In addition to its value as a readers' advisory guide, this book can serve as a key to building a core young adult fiction collection or as a guide to purchasing for a collection that is weak in some genres. The appendixes list professional and genre-specific reading resources, epic fantasy, and genre fiction for reluctant readers. Indexes are organized by title, subject, and author. Herald's resource is recommended for all libraries, especially those with smaller budgets.-Carlisle Webber.

Herz, Sarah K., and Donald R. Gallo. **From Hinton to Hamlet: Building Bridges Between Young Adult Literature and the Classics**, 2nd Ed., revised and expanded. Greenwood, 2005. 265p. PLB $41.95. 978-0-313-32452-9. Index. Biblio. **VOYA** February 2006.

The new edition of this professional classic addresses a need in many schools. Aimed at teachers and librarians, the text offers personal experiences, testimonials, data, and theory for incorporating young adult literature into classrooms. Early chapters, expanded and rewritten, describe Herz's experience "discovering" young adult literature and incorporating it into her classroom. These early chapters will be a resource for teachers and librarians arguing for the inclusion of young adult literature in their curriculum, although surveys and data cited are often dated, and some suggested strategies for convincing skeptical teachers and administrators of the worth of body of literature would be a great addition. More recent information on reading trends, in light of the rise in teen use of the Internet and the explosion in publishing for teens, would also be relevant and interesting.

Despite the value of the first half of the book, its true worth becomes apparent in the later chapters. The authors include suggestions for using young adult literature in the classroom, including a chapter listing commonly taught classics alongside young adult titles with shared themes. The authors outline the "theme connections" between works and provide lists of other recommended materials. Sample assignments and suggestions for new ways to teach literature are included. The authors also include suggestions for moving young adult literature out of the English classroom and across the curriculum and provide an extensive list of resources that provide more information about young adult books. This resource is a must-have for all school libraries and one to be considered for public libraries as well. Libraries that use the first edition would do well to consider purchasing the second. Although much of the information in the early chapters is similar, Herz and Gallo have updated their recommended young adult titles to include recently published books.-Anita Beaman.

Hill, Chrystie. **Inside, Outside, and Online: Building Your Library Community**. ALA Editions, 2009. 192p. $50 Trade pb. 978-0-8389-0987-4. Index. Biblio. Notes. Further Reading. Appendix. **VOYA** October 2009.

The process of community building in libraries using research-based assertions and practical examples is explored in this text. The author begins with the premise that a number of developments in recent years— including social science research, particularly on the notion of social capital, the Gates Foundation work to help libraries deliver public-access computing, and the developments in social computing forged by Web 2.0 technologies—have emerged to underscore the importance of libraries continuing to strive to create and strengthen community in order to be more effective, vibrant, and sustainable institutions. Hill argues that successful community building in libraries addresses five common practices, which are to assess, deliver, engage, iterate, and sustain. Chapters devoted to each of these areas include brief anecdotes from practitioners about how these principles are being used within their institutions. Guiding questions, research-based information, and examples from the field give each chapter a philosoph-ical basis as well as a practical approach.

Focused mostly on public libraries, the ideas and processes presented within the text are applicable for libraries of any type. In accessible ways replete with examples, the author lays a solid foundation for each of the highlighted areas including needs assess-ments, service offerings, communicating with users, evaluation, and building libraries for the future. Librarians will find this book inspiring and practical. Readers will begin to plan ways in which to act to strengthen the library community within their own insti-tutions as they turn the pages.—Erin Wyatt.

Hine, Thomas. **The Rise and Fall of the American Teenager**. Harper Perennial, 2000, ©1999. 336p. PLB $23. 978-1-4395-7358-7. $14.99 Trade pb. 978-0-380-72853-4. Index. Biblio. Further Reading. **VOYA** February 2000.

This sweeping and fascinating examination of the roles that teenagers have played in United States history, from the first settlers to the present, crosses societal, economic, political, and psychological lines. The words "rise" and "fall" in the title refer more to how society first invented "teenagers" and then changed its attitude toward teens—rather than to anything teenagers have done or not done. The author places research on adolescents in an interesting context, providing a complete "youth time line" while offering some fascinating ways of approaching and interpreting the best studies available. The uniqueness of the book lies in the author's perspective in looking at how teens were viewed and treated in each peri-od of American history, and the way Hine illustrates with copious quotes how economic and societal realities determined that view. By the time the author reaches the problems of youth today, readers are able to see how we arrived at this juncture and to understand the solutions Hine sets forth—whether or not we agree with them. A glance at the extensive list of sources used by Hine, including Daniel Offer, the Carnegie Council on Adolescent Development, Joseph Adelson, Mihaly Csikszentmihalyi, Joy Dryfoos, and Mary Pipher, reassures the reader that the author has indeed done his homework.

The book is designed to have popular appeal; the omission of footnotes or complete citations will be a problem for researchers. However those interested in or working with young adults and those who do public speaking and training will welcome the wealth of interesting facts, quotes, and viewpoints presented here. –Sue Rosenzweig.

Honnold, RoseMary, for the Young Adult Library Services Association (YALSA). **Get Connected: Tech Programs for Teens**. Neal-Schuman, 2007. 149p. $45 Trade pb. 978-1-55570-613-5. Index. Illus. Photos. Charts. Further Reading. Ap-pendix. **VOYA** October 2007.

This book is, without question, the one that every young adult librarian needs to add to their professional reading stack this year. Each chapter introduces a successful teen tech library program. Who can resist new programs that really work? One of the best things about this book is the contact information for the libraries and librarians who have hosted each program outlined in the book. If one gets stuck or wants first-hand information, one can go straight to the source. There is also further information listed for each chapter. The first section of the book is dedicated to fun. Covering programming for everything from gaming to podcasting to audio and video products, there is something for everyone. The real problem is deciding which program to start with-DDR competition or setting up a Fantasy Baseball League, digital art, or Japanese extravaganza. The second section concentrates on education, including some great ideas for database tutorials, information literacy-type mini-courses, and programs for specific skill building. Why not partner with a corporate sponsor to present a game design course, or have workshops dedicated to creating business cards? The third section is on encouraging one's teen group to get involved. Although young adult librarians all know the importance of this idea, the book brings concrete ways to involve youth in publicizing and recruiting for their own group.

Appendixes include a questionnaire for submitting a favorite teen tech program for the next **Get Connected**, an interpretation of the Library Bill of Rights for youth services librarians, another interpretation geared for electronic services, *Competencies for Librarians Serving Youth* report findings, and a toolkit for Librarians in Social Networking technologies. This resource is highly recommended for any librarian or teacher involved in planning youth programs.-Angie Hammond.

Hughes-Hassell, Sandra, and Violet H. Harada. **School Reform and the School Library Media Specialist**. Libraries Unlimited, 2007. 199p. $40 Trade pb. 978-1-59158-427-8. Index. Charts. Source Notes. **VOYA** April 2008.

Change is the constant in today's educational institutions, and this resource supplies the tools and methodology needed to enable school librarians to become skilled change agents. Media specialists' skills have evolved along with the role of the school library, making them uniquely qualified to be leaders and advocates for many types of educational metamorphoses. School librarians, researchers, and educators contribute chapters in five different sections of the book: Librarian as Change Agent; Partners in Student Achievement; Developing Literacy in the Twenty-First Century; Serving Diverse Student Populations; and Building Professionalism. The first chapter, "Change Agentry," is an inspirational reminder of the unique skill sets librarians possess that enable them to be leaders in the change process. The chapter about family literacy is another superb piece, offering suggestions for planning family literacy programs, providing Web sites, and listing recommended practices and funding sources. "Professional Development" gives excellent suggestions for building support in both the school and the community.

The authors provide an excellent resource for all school library media specialists. Every chapter deals with cutting-edge concerns for today's schools, and the authors deal with the topics in clear, concise prose, presenting constructive information and concrete examples. Most chapters contain helpful tables and charts; all have an extensive list of references. Whether a librarian wishes to become a change agent or wants to understand and effectively deal with change, this book is a superb information source.-Rachelle Bilz.

Intner, Carol F. **Homework Help from the Library: In Person and Online**. ALA Editions, 2010. 216p. $47. Oversize pb. 978-0-8389-1046-7. **VOYA** August 2011.

Not only is this basic reference readable and informative, it also contributes to the understanding between public librarians and school librarians. Building on the concept that information services and education converge with homework help, the author sketches in the history of youth services and current learning theories. She offers practical suggestions for needs assessment and determining a guiding philosophy. Speaking to the public librarian, Intner outlines the points to consider in designing a homework help program and training staff. Possible workshop topics include an overview of student needs and available resources, creating a comfortable and inviting space, considering the needs of different ages, understanding youth culture, and responding to various learning styles. An entire chapter is devoted to the role of technology in homework help. The author's discussion of interacting with students emphasizes good listening, positive attitude, and problem solving. Chapters on troubleshooting, marketing, and evaluating the program round out this offering.

Liberally sprinkled through the chapters are notes, references, and online tips; a table of goals from public libraries around the country follows the discussion of determining a philosophy. The simple surveys and other assessment tools described in the chapter on evaluating the homework help program stress patron feedback. Youth librarians will want this comprehensive and practical guide within easy reach.—Marla Unruh.

Jarrell, Jill S., and Tara C. Cannon. **Cooler Than Fiction: A Planning Guide for Teen Nonfiction Booktalks**. McFarland, 2010. 198p. $45. Oversize pb. 978-0-7864-4886-9. **VOYA** August 2011.

This wonderful professional resource for teen librarians and school media specialists focuses on the art of booktalking with a twist. This resource is available at a time when booktalking skills are more important than ever for librarians, and it covers nonfiction instead of fiction, an overlooked appeal for teens.     The authors' take on talking up nonfiction books to teens is refreshing and creative and shows their love of reading and teens. Each title receives a summary, along with extra discussion questions and activities for awesome interactive appeal. Each chapter groups an assortment of nonfiction titles into unique categories like "Funny, Gross, and Disturbing," "Food and Crafts," "Knowing Your World," "Science," and "History." Of particular highlight is the last chapter, "Interactives," which includes titles best used for openers and closers or breaks in the middle of a presentation. Each chapter summarizes the best ways to use each subject and apply titles in that area as booktalks. "Booktalking Resources" is also very helpful, listing many wonderful nonfiction titles that are great for booktalks, along with some professional resources recommended to polish skills.

This book is a much-needed tool for public librarians serving teens, as well as school media specialists, to develop excellent booktalking programs and partnerships while getting more teens to read and fun have doing so. It is a must-have for professional collections in public and school libraries.—Karen Sykeny.

Johnson, Doug. **School Libraries Head for the Edge: Rants, Recommendations, and Reflections**. Linworth/Libraries Unlimited/ABC-CLIO, 2009. 196p. $35 Trade pb. 978-1-58683-392-3. Illus. Source Notes. **VOYA** April 2010.

Johnson compiles many of the columns he wrote for **Technology Connection** and its successor, **Library Media Connection**, starting in 1995. Dividing the columns up by subject, Johnson offers chapters called "Libraries and Education in Transition"; "Professional Skills and Dispositions"; "Reading, Research, and Technology Skills"; "Technology in Libraries"; "Technology in Education"; Managing Good"; and "Determining Our Values." Within each chapter, he presents columns chronologically and follows each section with a "reflection." Johnson's overarching theme is that librarians must proactively take charge of their jobs—technology, instructional consulting, Internet use, copyright, promotion—or they and their libraries will be replaced. He offers many practical suggestions for taking action to prevent that eventuality.

This book is a quick and useful read. The short column length (around 800 words) makes it ideal for snatching a quick read between classes, and the complete table of contents makes it ideal for browsing by subject. Every column is concise, pithy, insightful, pragmatic, and laced with Johnson's wry humor. Although some of the older columns are showing their age and the author's promotion of the controversial "instructional consultant" role may ruffle some feathers, overall the book is a cornucopia of thoughtful and constructive ideas. Because Johnson works in the public school system, he targets their situations more often, but practitioners at all types of schools will find plenty of applicable information as well.—Rebecca Moore.

Johnson, Steve. **Digital Tools for Teaching: 30 E-Tools for Collaborating, Creating, and Publishing Across the Curriculum**. Maupin House, 2011. 136p. $23.95. Oversize pb. 978-1-934338-84-1. Glossary. Charts. Biblio, Appendix. **VOYA** April 2011.

Considering the vast number of e-tools now available, coupled with the fact that many of these tools are intimidating to some teachers, Johnson does an excellent job of sorting through them, listing his top choices, and even including ideas for using them. The book is divided into two parts. Part one provides information on today's tech-driven student, the importance of utilizing new technology, ways to start using the technology, and how to assess student products. Part two describes the e-tools, giving the following for each: a brief overview, how to get started, ways to use the tool in the classroom, and any other issues that need to be considered. Also included is an appendix that lists other recommended (but more content-specific) e-tools, the ISTE standards with an explanation of each, and a chart showing how the various e-tools mentioned meet the standards. Another helpful chart divides the tools into those for "newbies," "developing users," and "advanced users."

For many teachers simply covering the required content can be overwhelming, not to mention incorporating technology and ISTE standards. Digital Tools provides a wealth of information in a user-friendly, practical format that would benefit all educators regardless of grade level or content area. With easy-to-understand explanations and an avoidance of too much "tech speak," this book makes integrating technology a much more manageable, and much less intimidating, task. – Gina Bowling.

Jones, Patrick, and Joel Shoemaker. **Do It Right! Best Practices for Serving Young Adults in School and Public Libraries**. Neal-Schuman, 2001. 182p. $55 Trade pb. 978-1-55570-394-3. **VOYA** October 2001.

The philosophy that underlies this approach to best practices is a user-centered perspective of customer service that is built upon respect for young adults. The unique contribution of this book is in combining in one volume ways that both school and public libraries can serve teens better. Shoemaker describes how facility design, critical encounters between teens and staff, and school policies can affect customer service in the media center. Addressing best practices in public libraries, Jones discusses models of the different visions of YA services and writes how libraries "can create 'raving fans' out of teen customers." He adapts some pointers from the business world for improving service to teens. Both authors draw upon Mary K. Chelton's dissertation, *Adult-Adolescence Service Encounters: The Library Context* (Ph.D dissertation, Rutgers University, 1997) in which Chelton examines "the relationships between teens and adult providers in both public and school library contexts." In her introduction **Do It Right!**, Chelton explains the concept of customer service.

The two areas of school and public library services to teens are treated separately. Although school and public librarians serving youth have an opportunity here to read about the different perspectives of each other's work, there are some missed opportunities to integrate, at both conceptual and practical levels, a dialogue between them. One area in which the two services to teens converge is reflected in Jones's useful chapter on "Netting Pathfinders with Big6™." Jones outlines the main steps of the school-based research process model for librarians who serve teens in public libraries because of the relevance to homework assignments. Although Jones's work with schools and suggestions for working with teachers are interspersed in his authored chapters, cooperation between school and public libraries—an important extension to customer service—is not emphasized as a separate topic in this text.

One could have wished for more depth in Shoemaker's discussions of customer service in the school library media center and more mention of relevant research and recent contributions in areas such as facility design and student reference services. Although written from a customer perspective, much of the actual content is covered in greater depth elsewhere. Shoemaker does address, however, the crucial issue of "balance between freedom and control" that is faced by school library media specialists and how this balance is played out in library policies and institutional rules. A useful table sums up the purpose of policies and rules and their "unintended consequences." This issue rarely is addressed in texts for school library media specialists and is one that needs to be discussed critically in relation to good customer service.

This combined perspective is an inspiring text for both school and public librarians serving teens. One hope that it also will work to bring school and public libraries together in providing the best service to teens.—Hilary Crew.

Jones, Patrick, Maureen L. Hartman, and Patricia Taylor. **Connecting with Reluctant Teen Readers: Tips, Titles, and Tools**. Neal-Schuman, 2006. 314p. $59.95 Trade pb. 978-1-55570-571-8. Index. Biblio. **VOYA** February 2007.

For teachers and librarians working with teenagers, witnessing the transformation from reluctant reader to avid reader is one of life's sweetest triumphs. Youth who begin by professing that they "hate reading" end up pestering their young adult librarians for more and more suggestions. If one is looking for inspired ways to get more kids from the "hate reading" to the "love reading" stage, here is the perfect book. A masterful compilation of "tips, titles, and tools" is amassed from the expertise of YA librarians, teachers, and researchers across the country. As many professionals working with teens already suspect, there is no one model of reluctant teen reader, and thus no one remedy that will sweep everyone along the path of happy reading. In one chapter, four types of such readers are identified (dormant, uncommitted, unmotivated, and unskilled), and strategies for engaging each type are suggested. Elsewhere the professional tendency to classify certain kinds of reading (e.g. magazines, repair manuals) as substandard is examined. Are librarians consistently discouraging readers with their well-meaning guidance toward the same set of award-winning books? The entire second half of the book is devoted to booklists, the majority of which are annotated.

For most librarians and teachers, good readers' advisory starts with good recommendations, and this book includes more than 150 pages of suggested titles, all indexed by title, subject, and author. Go ahead and invest in this book to really make a difference in the reading lives of teenagers.-Diane Emge Colson.

Jones, Patrick, Michele Gorman, and Tricia Suellentrop. **Connecting Young Adults and Libraries: A How-to-Do-It Manual**, 3rd Ed. Neal-Schuman, 2004. 425p. Trade pb. 978-1-55570-508-4. O.P. Glossary. Index. Charts. Biblio. Appendix. **VOYA** February 2005.

It would be quite easy to build an entire library school course around this thoroughly revised edition. It is all here-from the theory behind developmental assets and how to serve young adults, to the practical sample surveys and forms that would work well in any community. The chapter "Collections" and its related bibliography at the back of the book would enable any library serving teens (or LST as referred to by the authors) to create a balanced, outstanding young adult collection on the first try. Some great new features in this edition include an entire chapter on programming and "The Language of the LST," a fifteen-page glossary of sorts that covers young adult librarian jargon all at once, including everything from common acronyms, such as for the Young Adult Library Services Association (YALSA), to important people in the field, such as Michael Cart.

Unfortunately there are many grammatical and spelling errors in this edition, which might enflame one's librarian sensibilities, but please do not throw out the baby with the bathwater. The information here is invaluable, especially to new librarians or for those who have learned all of this information piecemeal and for those who need a strengthening of resolve or an update of skills. Consider it an investment in continuing education for staff and one's self.-Melissa Potter.

Kane, Laura Townsend. **Working in the Virtual Stacks: the New Library & Information Science**. American Library Association, 2011. 184p. $47. Oversize pb. 978-0-8389-1103-7. Index. Notes. **VOYA** February 2012.

This sequel to **Straight From the Stacks: A Firsthand Guide to Careers in Library and Information Science** (American Library Association, 2003) examines changes in the careers of the now-termed "information professionals" in the digital age.

Through interviews with thirty-four librarians, the author describes backgrounds, training, environment, responsibilities, and the joys and frustrations of specialists in areas as diverse as veterinary medicine, Web design, and marketing. She groups them into five broad categories: subject specialists, technology gurus, social networkers, teacher and community liaisons, entrepreneurs, and administrators. Far from dry, the two- to three-page interviews read like conversations and are both entertaining and informative, intended to spark interest among those who have never before considered librarianship as a career choice.

Laura Townsend Kane is assistant director for information services at the University of South Carolina's School of Medicine. She has written a number of professional articles and books and is a highly qualified practitioner. Published by the prestigious American Library Association, including notes and a detailed index, this small handbook is a useful addition to the professional bookshelf.—Laura Woodruff.

Kane, Sharon. **Integrating Literature in the Content Areas: Enhancing Adolescent Learning and Literacy**. Holcomb Hathaway, 2008. 336p. $38 Trade pb. 978-1-890871-80-2. Index. Illus. Photos. Charts. Biblio. Further Reading. **VOYA** August 2009.

Packed with suggestions and resources for every teacher, this curriculum treasure chest illustrates how to integrate young adult literature so that students learn content, improve literacy, and enjoy reading—for life. The first two chapters justify emotionally accessible texts as central teaching tools and present an overview of teaching methods. The remaining chapters target genres: informational; fiction; biography, autobiography, and memoir; poetry; and how-to and hands-on. The first two parts of each genre chapter present a rationale, specific lesson plans, and "Walk-Throughs" that illustrate hands-on implementation. Kane's creative suggestions for discussion, study, research, and cooperative learning range from double-entry journals and graphic organizers to scrapbooking. The third section focuses on outstanding authors, such as James Cross Giblin, Walter Dean Myers, Naomi Shihab Nye, and Robert Sabuda. It also includes a full bibliography of the author's works and Web sites. Part four annotates books, tagged for age level, with booktalks targeted primarily to teachers and organized by content areas: Art; English/Language Arts; Languages and Cultures; Math and Technology; Music; Physical Education, Health, and Wellness; Science; Social Studies/History. Character booktalks, sprinkled through the bibliography, hold appeal for a student audience.

Kane emphasizes that cross-curriculum reading encourages lifelong education and that motivating content and process support both curiosity and high test scores. Every school, library, and teacher-training program should have at least one copy, and a young adult program planner or group leader will find it a fantastic and fascinating resource.—Lucy Schall.

Karp, Jesse. **Graphic Novels in Your School Library**. Illus. by Rush Kress. American Library Association, 2011. 160p. $50 Oversize pb. 978-0-8389-1089-4. Illus. Further Reading. Biblio. Index. **VOYA** June 2012.

Karp has created an inclusive resource for school librarians interested in adding the graphic novel format to their collections or expanding an existing collection. Illustrations assist in defining concepts and terminology. The book is divided into four parts: "The Form" describes graphic novels, analyzes the structure, and explains how the format is gaining wide respect as a literacy tool; "A History of American Sequential Art" presents an overview of comic books and graphic novels; "Annotated Reading Lists" recommends titles for preschool through twelfth grade; and "Lesson Plans and Activities" provides learning experiences organized by grade level.

The author has imparted a college course of material between two covers in an easily understood presentation. While wildly popular with students, manga, comic books, and graphic novels can be intimidating to many adults unfamiliar with this format. Karp's chapter on how graphic novels work will have even novices armed to discuss how writers and illustrators use subtle and detailed drawings to demonstrate the passage of time, action, and emotion. He successfully makes a case for the use of graphic novels in teaching reading, citing the complexities of the format that a reader must interpret and understand: "In every case, graphic novels build skills, confidence, and desire to move on to other formats and to continue reading just for the sake of enjoyment." The annotated booklists are invaluable and cover a wide selection of genres. The lesson plans and activities are perfect for librarian and teacher collaborations. This resource is a terrific addition for school and public libraries. The cover alone may have your students clamoring for a look as well.—Jeanine Fox.

Karten, Toby J. **Inclusion Strategies That Work for Adolescent Learners!** Corwin, 2009. 230p. $75.95. 978-1-4129-7045-7. $35.95 Trade pb. 978-1-4129-7046-4. Index. Charts. Biblio. **VOYA** June 2009.

Pragmatic, well-researched, and accessible, this book functions as a field guide for the educator motivated (or mandated) to create a classroom where meaningful educational experiences can be offered to middle and high school students of varying backgrounds and abilities. Conversational in tone, the many reference charts, graphic organizers, worksheets, suggested activities, and assessment rubrics make this a resource helpful to both beginning and seasoned educators. The author's understanding of the unique cognitive and physical characteristics of the adolescent helps validate the various inclusion strategies and teaching techniques suggested. The classroom teacher will appreciate the concept of instruction that differentiates to individual student needs but remains valid to all learners. The realistic acknowledgment that providing meaningful inclusionary instruction is time consuming, purposeful, and rewarding but works best when corroborated by a accommodating administrative and support staff prepares the teacher for the challenges of implementing these instructional methods in the classroom.

The "what" and "why" of including special needs students in the mainstream classroom is addressed well; however, it is the author's recommendations on "how" to implement classroom management, long-range planning, assessment options, and grading that prove to be the most valued aspect of this text. The eight stand-alone chapters, easy-to-read graphics, relevant Web site addresses, detailed bibliography, and comprehensive index make this text a helpful reference tool.—Lynne Farrell Stover.

Katz, Jon. **Geeks: How Two Lost Boys Rode the Internet out of Idaho**. Villard, 2000. 208p. PLB $23. 978-1-4352-9529-2. $14.95 Trade pb. 978-0-7679-0699-9. **VOYA**, *The View from VOYA*, April, 2000.

Katz had been writing for some time about the burgeoning computer Geek culture. Jesse Dailey and Eric Twilegar's candid email responses to an interview for a **Rolling Stone** article launched a relationship that led to this book. They helped Katz define Geeks, not only in terms of their immense Net knowledge, but as alienated from mainstream culture. Geeks are anarchists, libertarians, citizens only of the Net. Geeks despise authority, rejecting the educational and social structure that is suspicious of their smarts. Instead they form their own subculture on the Internet, "the freest part of American culture."

Katz covers the story of Dailey and Twilegar's migration from their home in Idaho to a new life in Chicago fraught with the pitfalls of their social ineptitude, and Katz's evolution into a role of mentorship. Youth advocates will identify with Katz as he wanders boundaries between advice and pushing, resists offering money, and comes to value Jesse so deeply that he puts himself on the line to get him into college.

**Geeks** is required reading for all who seek insight into teen culture, and inspiration to change the society that makes it so tough for our most gifted youth to survive. Exhorting us to "begin the work of restructuring American schools," Katz places "at the very top of the agenda: Freedom from abuse, humiliation, and cruelty."—Catherine Dunn MacRae

Kaye, Cathryn Berger. **Complete Guide to Service Learning: Proven, Practical Ways to Engage Students in Civic Responsibility, Academic Curriculum, and Social Action**. Free Spirit, 2004. 240p. Trade pb. 978-1-57542-133-9. O.P. Index. Illus. Forms. **VOYA** October 2004.

Kaye makes it sound so easy in this wonderful step-by-step guide to creating a service learning program in K-12 schools. She starts with an explanation of what constitutes a service learning activity, making a strong argument for service learning being a much more positive and proactive program than the typical community service programs that many schools endorse. Kaye creates fabulous forms and handouts to guide the reader in developing a program from the idea stage to the implementation stage. She provides some great examples of how service learning can lead to curriculum integration as well as some handy tips and practical advice on how to make the program flourish. Not only does Kaye offer sample areas where service learning programs can be successful—such as working with the elderly, homeless people, and those with AIDS—but she also provides fiction titles that exemplify service learning in a specific area. The excitement of reading a book that correlates to the service learning project they are working on will capture students' imaginations and illustrate how school is relevant to their everyday existence.

Kay provides an outstanding resource to guide educators in making ideas grow to be actions. If one is working with a service learning program or is trying to start one, this title is a must-have for the professional bookshelf.-Lori Matthews.

Kepler, Ann, Ed. **The ALA Book of Library Grant Money, Eighth Edition**. American Library Association, 2012. 448p. $175. Oversize pb. 978-0-8389-1058-0. Index. **VOYA** June 2012.

With tightening budgets, reduced staff, and sometimes even cut hours, libraries in America are suffering under the pressure of underfunding. Funding has become a huge issue for libraries, and many librarians are looking for seed money for beginning new endeavors or maintaining already established projects. Librarians experienced with searching for grants will find the eighth edition of this book well organized and of great use in their search; those with less experience or new to grants will find this printed guide an excellent companion to online research.

Laid out in a dictionary-style format, grants are arranged alphabetically by the name of the foundation or organization sponsoring the grant. Profiles of funders are provided as well, with the information gathered from reliable sources, including the IRS and the funders' websites. The profiles contain as much information as possible, including typical grant recipients, past recipients, application procedures, and the website where the grant can be found online. If a librarian is looking for a specific grant, the book's four indices can help narrow down the search. This is a tool that should be on the resource shelves of librarians and libraries who are preparing and planning for their future and the future of all libraries. Library funding may never return to the levels it previously reached, so any extra help by those funders willing to give to libraries is needed and welcomed.—Amanda Fensch.

Klein, Jesse. **The Bully Society**. New York University Press, 2012. 318p. $29.95. 978-0-8147-4888-6. Index. **VOYA** June 2012.

A scholarly, insightful commentary on aggression and violence within peer groups, Klein's treatise surveys an everyday misery for youths targeted for ridicule, exclusion, racism, and assault and proposes intelligent, compassionate methods to end persecution. Ten chapters examine bullying issues from the perspective of social science—socioeconomic class, gender, sexuality, adult intimidation, cultural forms of socialization and discipline, and inhumane institutions and electronic communication that condone and encourage harassment. Essential to Klein's discussion, repressive microcosms within schools and playgroups inflict harsh reprisals for individuals who reject coercion by the majority. Analysis cites headline examples, from Columbine High School in Colorado and Robert Steinhäuser's murder of sixteen people in Erfurt, Germany, to New Jersey's 2011 Anti-Bullying Bill of Rights. Klein's solutions speak to the entire educational environment—assessment-heavy schools, jock coddling, homophobia, mean-spirited authority figures, the "smart girl" syndrome, and fundamentalism and the "gay agenda." Using comparisons of innovative programs in American and European schools, she recommends collective courage programs, whole-school eradication of bullying, compassionate culture, and nonviolent communication.

Useful to the parent, teacher, coach, counselor, principal, or librarian, the topic-subtopic division of the index points to analysis of specific questions: cyberbullying, suicide, cliques, hazing, sexual harassment, the National Rifle Association, Facebook, gang rape, and the It Gets Better Project, which publishes anecdotal models of past successes in overcoming interpersonal trauma. This title is highly recommended for professional shelves and teacher training courses.—Mary Ellen Snodgrass.

Klor, Ellin, and Sarah Lapin. **Serving Teen Parents: From Literacy to Life Skills**. Libraries Unlimited, 2012. 200p. $45. Oversize pb. 978-1-59884-693-5. Index. Photos. Source Notes. Appendixes. **VOYA** June 2012.

This comprehensive guide successfully shows how libraries can support teen parents and their children. Librarians are shown how to develop, implement, and evaluate services and programs for teen parents and their children. Chapters cite research studies and provide references at the conclusion. A wide variety of topics are covered, well beyond what one may think of when considering services to provide to teen parents. The authors demonstrate what it takes to provide these services, discussing partnerships, planning, training, funding, and more. Most useful, they also include brief overviews of teen parent programs in the United States. Some chapters offer examples of programs that focus just on teens, with matters like literacy skills, financial advice, and job searches, while others outline ideas for both parents and their children, like playing at the library, offering plans for crafts, exercise, leisure, and more. The chapter on interactive literacy programs is invaluable. Here, librarians will find extensive outlines for story times, covering everything from choosing books and songs to reproducible fingerplays and flannelboard patterns.

An appendix provides reproducible materials of surveys, handouts, and question-naires. It is difficult to imagine anything the authors left out of this guide. The many useful models and plans for each piece of the programming make the guide easy to use for libraries just starting to provide these services. Though at times the book is intimidatingly dense, by providing a thorough examination of teenage parents and their lives, the authors give librarians a well-rounded view into the complex needs of this population.—Amanda MacGregor.

Krashen, Stephen D. **The Power of Reading: Insights from the Research**, 2nd Ed. Libraries Unlimited with Heinemann, 2004. 199p. $27 Trade pb. 978-1-59158-169-7. Index. Biblio. Source Notes. **VOYA** June 2005.

As he did in his original edition (1992/ **VOYA** October 1993), Krashen discusses "The Research," "The Cure," and "Other Issues and Conclusions" that make a strong case for the value of free reading in children's literacy development. More than two hundred additional references, not all new, with sixty-four dating before the publication of the first edition, supplement the substantially revised text. A fifth of the new citations refer to studies in which Krashen was involved. The studies focused heavily on middle school students but covered children from kindergarten through high school as well. Of particular interest to school and public libraries is the expanded section on access that differentiates between classroom, school, and public libraries. Krashen maintains that "if free voluntary reading is the only way to develop adequate levels of reading com-prehension, writing style, vocabulary," etc., then "the most obvious step is to provide access to books." The information on school libraries includes conclusions from Keith Curry Lance's groundbreaking studies on the impact of school library media programs.

Powerful quotes for both school and public libraries for making a case with funders can be found in this chapter.

Readers should know that not all experts agree with Krashen's conclusions. The National Reading Panel Report (NICHD, 2000) claims that the kinds of studies cited by Krashen were "correlational in nature, and correlation does not imply causation." Krashen has publicly taken issue with the National Reading Panel's conclusions but makes mention of the report and his criticism of it here only in the chapter notes. Although the structure and conclusions remain essentially the same, inclusion of studies performed in the twelve years since publication of the first book make the second worth purchasing. All teachers, librarians, and anyone interested in the reading development of children, young adults, and ESL students will benefit from reading this book.-Linda Williams, Guest Reviewer.

Kunzel, Bonnie, and Constance Hardesty. **Teen-Centered Book Club: Readers into Leaders**. Libraries Unlimited, 2006. 213p. $40 Trade pb. 978-1-59158-193-2. Index. Source Notes. Appendix. **VOYA** April 2007.

This complete and comprehensive guide to planning and running successful and relevant teen book clubs begins with sensible and practical information about teens as readers and group participants, plus what constitutes effective and well-prepared adult book-club leaders and advisors for teens. What teens want and need from their particular book club and advice on allowing them to take the lead in decision making and club operation are carefully covered. A wide selection of conventional and innovative book club ideas is described, with details on developing them and examples of books that could be used for each. The choices include such ideas as theme or genre clubs, reading/writing clubs, blogging groups, and bookchatters, where everyone reads a different book. Valuable suggestions are given on how to publicize and promote the clubs. Very specific and extremely wise and useful advice on arranging meetings, getting to know the teens, selecting books, creating questions, and facilitating discussions is provided. Activities to further explore and connect teens to the books incorporate dance, art, poetry, music, and reader's theater. The last section tells how to evaluate the book club for pertinent results and to use this information for reinforcement and/or improvement.

This guide is meticulously organized, carefully researched, and highly readable with practical elements that can be readily applied. In contrast, **Teen Book Discussion Groups @ the Library** by Constance B. Dickerson (Neal-Schuman, 2004/ **VOYA** February 2005) gives only basic rather than extensive information on planning and running groups. It is strong, however, in providing a wide selection of suggested books and questions to consider, and would serve as a good complement to Kunzel and Hardesty's title. The high caliber experience and knowledge from the long and illustrious YA services and writing careers of both Kunzel and Hardesty is reflected in this important contribution to the body of professional resources for those working with teens, books, and reading in schools, libraries, and other settings.-Diane Tuccillo.

Landsman, Julie. **A White Teacher Talks about Race**. Scarecrow Education, 2001. 169p. PLB $28.95. 978-1-4352-9411-0. $19.95 Trade pb. 978-1-57886-181-1. References. **VOYA** October 2001.

Leading readers through one composite day of teaching, Landsman focuses on high school students and their complicated lives who attend an academic support program in Minneapolis. In introducing the reader to her multicultural students—African American, Asian American, Latino, Native American, and white—she shares glimpses of their lives as they come in and out of her classroom. Some are involved with drugs, some are teen mothers, others have spent time in prison, and one young woman is homeless, but all are endeavoring to complete high school. As participant observer through her first-person, freely flowing narrative, Landsman draws readers in, enabling them to see her students and to hear the hopes, fears, difficulties, and triumphs as the teens interact with each other and with their teacher. The students' voices bring their personal perspectives to bear upon issues surrounding race and education, including how they contend with peers who attempt to dissuade them from going back to classes.

Landsman writes frankly about the intersections of race, culture, class, gender, education, and white privilege. Too often, she writes, there is a refusal to talk about race or racial differences, but this is a cop-out. She writes about the need for inclusive classrooms and curricula. "Is it too much to encompass the mixture of all these kids' lives, in what they read, in whom they see?" Landsman, writing from the standpoint of a white teacher, acknowledges her own mistakes and assumptions in dealing with issues of race and difference so that others might learn. She points out the inequities of an educational system wherein there are schools in which "the only gifted program is a white program." Landsman's reflections have import for all who teach and work with teens.—Hilary Crew.

Langemack, Chapple. **The Booktalker's Bible: How to Talk About the Books You Love to Any Audience**. Libraries Unlimited, 2003. 176p. $30 Trade pb. 1-56308-944-0. Index. Biblio. Further Reading. Appendix. **VOYA** December 2003.

Langemack provides a superb one-volume how-to-do-it book that covers anything a novice would need to know and some things of which experienced booktalkers might need reminding, without really duplicating any other book. Within fourteen chapters, she covers basics such as "why do it"; "knowing your audience" with specific chapters on adults and kids; choosing your books"; and more, but she also includes material on evaluation, what to take on the road when going out to talk, booktalking in schools, and variations such as hand-selling, peer booktalks, and media talks. She enlivens the text with many boxed personal anecdotes of booktalk situations that worked or did not from contributors other than herself and includes a variety of personal experiences, not all of them great, to let readers know that she, too, has had to learn a lot the hard way. She includes booktalking issues including memorization, handling disruptions, what to wear, and controversial titles in schools.

Beyond its utter practicality, the book is really hilarious in spots and a good, interesting read. For example, in the chapter on booktalking to children and teens, Langemack says, "It's a fact of life that the best way to grab and hold the attention of nine-to-twelve-year-old boys (and girls) is to gross them out. I'm not suggesting you make fart noises with your armpits, although I'm sure if you wanted instruction in this technique, this is a group that would be glad to oblige." This wonderful, engaging book is a great addition to the arsenal of tools librarians serving young adults need to have—and use.—Mary K. Chelton.

Langhorne, Mary-Jo, and Denise Rehmke, with the Iowa City Community School District. **Developing 21st Century Literacies**. Neal-Schuman, 2011. 300p. $75. Oversize pb. 978-1-55570-752-1. Index. Further Reading. **VOYA** April 2012.

This title will be a welcome addition to the professional collection of many school librarians and administrators. It achieves its stated purpose well: "to provide a model for school librarians who seek to develop and implement a sound library curriculum in their own schools and districts." While it could easily serve as a text for preservice teacher-librarians, it will also be of value to more veteran librarians, especially those in small or single-school districts who have little chance to collaborate with others. Those without access to colleagues will benefit from the collaborative efforts of the librarians behind this blueprint. The plan presented is just that, a blueprint of a single district's library curriculum, and does not purport to be a universal curriculum. Even so, it provides an excellent starting point for those without a formalized library curriculum or those without district leaders who understand the intricacies of how a library curriculum in the twenty-first century should be developed. It includes plans to be used for both fixed and flexible schedules, and elementary as well as secondary lessons. From an introductory discussion of twenty-first-century literacies and a comparison of differing national and state standards, to chapters on backward design, inquiry-based learning, assessment, sample lessons, and more, the authors have also included numerous links to the Iowa City Community School District library website, with access to additional dynamic content connected to the book.

Thanks to the many practicing librarians who collaborated on this book, it assumes the school librarian is an expert in many arenas essential to student success—inquiry process, research tools and methods, literature, reading comprehension and curriculum development, to name a few—a welcome stance in the current culture of shrinking budgets and job uncertainty. Those who are planning on revising, examining, or writing a library curriculum will benefit from this blueprint in supporting twenty-first-century students who "will need to be skillful readers, critical thinkers, creative innovative workers, and responsible citizens in a world that will be ever more global."—Rochelle Garfinkel.

Lerch, Maureen T., and Janet Welch. **Serving Homeschooled Teens and Their Parents**. Libraries Unlimited, 2004. 242p. $42 Trade pb. 978-0-313-32052-1. Index. Charts. Biblio. Source Notes. Further Reading. Appendix. **VOYA** February 2005.

This comprehensive toolbox for serving this often overlooked population is written by parties on both sides of the homeschool issue. Lerch, a librarian who overcame preconceived notions about homeschoolers, and Welch, a homeschooler who has a background in libraries, offer unique perspectives here. Lerch addresses prejudices that might block outreach, such as feeling that parents are incapable of teaching their children and fear of censorship issues from those with strong religious convictions. Welsh presents the other side, talking about what families really expect from their public library. A plan for establishing basic goals and different types of services and resources is presented through a series of forms, charts, and bibliographies, some with a religious slant. Because religious beliefs often add to the feelings of "differentness" that all teens have and contribute to the reason that many homeschooled teens do not participate in general teen programs, ideas are presented on how to draw in this audience and market for greatest impact. Many resources are needed to serve this population and the authors include recommended suppliers, periodicals, and Web sites to supplement an existing collection. Services that might have the most appeal to home-educating families, such as library tours, research instruction, and proctoring are highlighted.

There is an extensive resource list of curriculum publishers, statewide homeschool organizations and state departments of education, online testing sites, distance learning sources, online magazines, and core collections. Also included are impressive further reading recommendations and a guide to creating one's own homeschool handbook. It is a much-needed resource highly recommended for all libraries.-Arlene Garcia.

Lesesne, Teri S. **Making the Match: The Right Book for the Right Reader at the Right Time, Grades 4 through 12**. Stenhouse, 2003. 232p. $21 Trade pb. 1-57110-381-3. Biblio. Appendix. *The View from VOYA*, **VOYA** April 2004.

Librarians would call this topic readers' advisory; teachers call it reading motivation. In her introduction, it sounds simple: "Making the match between book and reader relies on knowledge in three areas: knowing the reader, knowing the book, and knowing the techniques and strategies for bringing book and reader together." Avid reader Lesesne wondered why many of her middle school students declared, "I have never found a book I like"—even when they had good reading skills. This "verbal gauntlet" challenged her to delve into what made each "gauntlet thrower" tick. Just one question could work wonders: "If an author could write a perfect book for you, what would it be like?" Lesesne asked. Usually she could produce such a book—the student simply didn't know where to look, and no one had ever asked what this young reluctant reader was looking for.

Three sections cover the three ingredients for matchmaking. "Knowing the Kids" describes what adults must learn about teens' cultural and personal milieu. Her lucid description of adolescents' physical, mental, emotional and social development relates directly to their reading needs. The ""Knowing the Books" section empowers any teacher or librarian to navigate the world of YA literature for the reviews, awards, listservs, websites, booklists, and types of books that work best for teens. In the final "Making the Match" section, Lesesne explores the stages in the development of lifetime readers, from the "unconscious delight" of getting lost in a book to reading for other purposes: autobiographical, vicarious experience, philosophical speculation, and aesthetic experience.

What a perfect weapon this book will be in the battle to improve school summer reading lists—or better yet, a peace pipe that public and school librarians can share with teachers as they craft excellent lists of teen appeal together.—Catherine Dunn MacRae.

Lesesne, Teri. **Naked Reading: Uncovering What Tweens Need to Become Lifelong Readers**. Stenhouse, 2006. 118p. $16 Trade pb. 978-1-57110-416-8. Charts. Notes. Further Reading. Appendix. **VOYA** October 2006.

Many happy childhood readers find themselves disenchanted with reading when they reach adolescence. It is an especially rough time to lose touch with the solace of reading because young adolescents often feel alone and alienated. Lucky young readers encounter an adult like Teri Lesesne, who well understands both the mindset of early adolescents and the myriad of books written for that age group. Lesesne examines obstacles that divert tweens from the company of books. She begins by looking at the psychological needs of adolescents, making helpful book suggestions that might target these needs. For example, Lesesne sites the work of Kantrowitz and Springen, who compiled a list of qualities essential for adolescent development called the Five Cs (competence, confidence, connection, character, and caring). Lesesne matches books with each of these qualities. Competence, for example, is matched with Chasing Vermeer, Love That Dog, Drawing Lessons, Matchit, and Sparks. This insightful connection between appropriate psychological development and specific young adult titles is one of the elements that makes this book essential for middle school teachers and librarians.

Most of the book is targeted toward teachers, with numerous ways to prescribe reading assignments and suggestions for motivating students. But anyone with an interest in connecting tweens with literature will find inspiration here. Lesesne really knows her books. A lengthy appendix includes approximately 200 books suitable for middle school students, with annotations. Lesesne's zeal for her subject is highly infectious, making it a must-read for anyone working with tweens.-Diane Emge Colson.

Lesesne, Teri. **Reading Ladders: Leading Students from Where They Are to Where We'd Like Them to Be**. Heinemann, 2010. 144p. $18.95. 978-0-325-01726-6. Biblio. Appendix. Index. **VOYA** December 2010.

This excellent book will help teachers and librarians guide students to books along a continuum that will encourage them to tackle more challenging and complex reading material. Lesesne explains the steps in building lifelong readers from a solid foundation of reading aloud, access to books and models of literacy, to having time to read. She then discusses what motivates students in choosing books to read and how to use these variables to encourage more reading. Book variables such as title, cover, form, and genre—along with such student variables as gender and age—can be used to guide students to the next "right" book for them.

"A reading ladder is a series or set of books that are related in some way (e.g., thematically) and that demonstrate a slow, gradual development from simple to complex." Lesesne's readable style is clear and concise, making it easy to understand how to construct reading ladders. She gives many examples, with reasons for her choices to aid in understanding. Her discussion of assessment gives many ideas for activities that will show how students have learned from their reading. The appendix lists possible themes for reading ladders. This is an important book for all teachers and librarians who are looking for ways to encourage students' reading development.—Deborah L. Dubois.

Lesko, Wendy Schaetzel. **Maximum Youth Involvement: The Complete Game-plan for Community Action**. Youth Activism Project (P. O. Box E, Kensington, MD 20895), Rev. ed., 2003. 170p. $35 + shipping (bulk discounts available); (800) KIDPOWER or *http://www.youthactivism.com*. **VOYA**, *The View from VOYA*, June 2003.

Lesko's flexible, how-to-do-it **Gameplan** works for teen community action campaigns from antismoking to gun control. Facillitating collaboration between adults and youths in a variety of circumstances, it easily translates to library settings. Inspiring and practical tips appear under headings in question form, in sections from Youth Recruitment and Retention ("What about mixing age groups or youths from different backgrounds?") to Advocacy Skill-Building Activities ("What icebreakers encourage group focus on advocacy?") Valuable reproducible forms in the appendix enhance planning and training. For our library budget crisis, start with "Who's Who in City/County Government Worksheet."

Lesko distills years of activism and training into lucid, accessible road maps for countless situations. Her tone is encouraging but forthright, counseling how to handle possible pitfalls. She explores the terrain that can intimidate newcomers to youth involvement—role playing exercises help each generation reveal its stereotypes of the other. Quietly radical observations could only come from experience: "Sometimes there is a real advantage for not knowing the 'adult way' of doing things so that young people invent . . . new tactics."

Lesko's expert guidance in "effective intergenerational advocacy" will help young adult librarians to re-evaluate our convictions about working with teens and about where libraries stand on youth development. Then we can co-create libraries with our young people—libraries so responsive and essential that our teen public won't allow their services to be cut.—Catherine Dunn MacRae.

Lukenbill, W. Bernard, and Barbara Froling Immroth. **Health Information in a Changing World: Practical Approaches for Teachers, Schools, and School Librarians**. Libraries Unlimited, 2010. 244p. $45. Oversize pb. 978-1-59884-398-9. Index. Illus. Photos. Maps. Source Notes. Further Reading. Appendix. **VOYA** December 2010.

Librarians typically select resources for other people. This resource recognizes the role of the librarian in the education of youth and provides tools for librarians, teachers, and administrators to develop a skills-based curriculum that will empower students through health literacy and awareness of healthy behavior. Holistic health integrates mind and body and extends from personal health to health-care systems and global concerns. Specific instructional strategies, rubrics for the assessment of outcomes, and examples of alignment with national standards provide a framework for a curriculum. Activities are provided for different age levels. Locating and evaluating resources are significant components in developing health literacy. This toolkit includes discussion of such techniques as Boolean logic to search databases and procedures to evaluate information for accuracy and bias. Instructional strategies utilize health themes in biography, folklore, and global concerns to develop skills in problem solving and critical thinking across the curriculum. Activities such as health fairs or community demonstrations connect the student, family, and community.

Extensive listings of health information from specific Web sites or printed material from organizations and programs make this a handy manual. This is quite an impressive book and a real treasure for any professional involved with health education, whether for the classroom, public health, or personal counseling.—Marilyn Brien.

MacKellar, Pamela, and Stephanie Gerdin. **Winning Grants: A How-To-Do-It Manual for Librarians with Multimedia Tutorials and Grant Development Tools**. Neal-Schuman, 2010. 275p. $99.95 Oversize pb. 978-1-55570-700-2. Glossary. Index. Illus. Photos. Charts. Biblio. DVD. **VOYA** December 2010.

Winning Grants is a useful how-to manual especially focused on libraries that are looking for funding for particular projects. Part I details the steps necessary to create a winning grant proposal for public or school libraries. It stresses the importance of early planning that includes the vision and mission of the library, from which any grant proposal must grow. It shows how to do a needs assessment and how to build goals and objectives that are important to your particular community and library. It stresses the need to involve a planning team and community partners to build a stronger grant and to be sure the plan meets the community's needs. It repeats the importance of writing the grant based on needs, rather than writing a grant because money is available.

Part II includes real-life stories of projects that won grants. These stories can be used to inspire ideas for your own library or to look at the process the grant winners went through and their advice to other grant seekers. Part III contains templates for planning tools such as checklists and worksheets. These can also be found on a multi-media DVD which includes instructional videos that go along with each chapter. The tools are extremely helpful because they are easy to access and print multiple times. While the book focuses on libraries, the grant development methods could be applied to other groups who are trying to write a grant or organize a large project. Following each of the steps would benefit any planner.—Cindy Faughnan.

MacKeller, Pamela H. **Writing Successful Technology Grant Proposals: A LITA Guide**. Neal-Shuman, 2012. 220p. $70 Oversize pb. 978-1-55570-763-7. Appendixes. Index. **VOYA** August 2012.

This expansive manual details seven steps in the grant-writing process. Although it focuses on technology grants, a librarian could modify the process to suit individual needs for virtually any type of grant application. The guide advocates an in-depth approach to grant writing, starting with planning. This step includes conducting a community-needs assessment to determine which resources would best serve library users and the broader community. From there, the process moves to project design, teamwork, and research before the actual grant writing begins. According to the book, many people skip the initial steps and rush right to the grant application; this often leads to an unsuccessful, sour experience. Following this guide takes time, but the extensive steps outlined here should, in the long run, save librarians from headache and failure.

After winning the grant, the process does not stop. MacKeller includes project implementation steps and review in the process, which then cycles back to the beginning as the librarian begins planning all over again. Although dense, this text presents excellent information and has a strong patron focus: grants are not about objects or money—they are about people. The appendixes include sample grant applications and resources that will be useful in every step of the grant-writing process.—Jennifer McConnel.

Magid, Larry, and Anne Collier. **MySpace Unraveled: A Parent's Guide to Teen Social Networking**. Peachpit Press, 2007. 184p. Trade pb. 978-0-321-48018-7. O. P. Illus. **VOYA** December 2006.

What a breath of fresh air! This book does not buy into the fear and hype associated with **MySpace** and other social networking sites. Instead it is a positive look at what **MySpace** is, why teens use it, and what parents should know to help guarantee that their teen is safe when using **MySpace** or other social networking sites. Magid and Collier take a step-by-step approach to the topic. After explaining what **MySpace** and social networking is, the authors let the parents know how to set up a **MySpace** account, describe how each of the features (adding friends, music, IMing, and so on) work, and even explain how to keep track of a teen's activity on **MySpace** with special Web services and software. The theme all the way through is that it is a parent's responsibility to know what's going on with **MySpace**. Inserted throughout the book are sections labeled "Key Parenting Point." These sections highlight features of **MySpace** and social networking to which parents should pay particular attention. For example, the authors point out that teens should not share their **MySpace** calendars. These "Key Points" do a good job of highlighting some of the features that parents might miss or might not think too much about. By stressing these issues, the authors give parents jumping-off points for talking with their teens about safe use of social networking technologies.

The book is easy to read, filled with colorful screenshots, and sure to help parents understand what their role is in their teen's involvement in social networking. With this title in the collection, librarians will have a quality resource to recommend to parents who are wondering about social networking and concerned about its impact on teen life. –Linda W. Braun, *Guest Reviewer.*

Mahood, Kristine. **A Passion for Print: Promoting Reading and Books to Teens**. Libraries Unlimited, 2006. 224p. $40 Trade pb. 978-1-59158-146-8. Index. Photos. Biblio. Further Reading. Appendix. **VOYA** December 2006.

Impressive in its organization and depth of information, this great resource covers practically everything young adult for the public or high school librarian. Starting out with research-based teen studies, Mahood then couples this information with studies from such diverse fields as marketing, merchandising, and graphic design to bring teen service into focus in the library. Balancing the needs and desires of teens with the mission of the library, this book covers teen assumptions about reading, teens as consumers, collection development, designing a teen space, creating book displays, print promotions, Web-page design, readers' advisory, booktalking, and planning literature-centered activities. Chapters have an easy flow, with each topic carefully introduced and attentively explored. Mahood comfortably incorporates a thought-provoking combination of philosophical and practical application. Further reading offered at the end of each chapter entices the reader to glean more insight into the selected topic. The table of contents is very clear and concise if one is looking for specific information, but the reader may just find this resource a stimulating exploration from cover to cover.

The book does what it sets out to do-help young adult librarians to find ways to promote reading and books to teens. The authors' passion for print and for teens is evident in the writing and the research that has been done to pull this handy little book together. One can strongly recommended it to seasoned veterans trying to keep on top of current trends or new young adult librarians interested in finding ways to guide teens to literature or literature to teens. Order one for work and another one to keep at home.-Angie Hammond.

**Managing the Internet Controversy**. Mark Smith, Ed. Neal-Schuman, 2001. 226p. $59.95 Trade pb. 978-1-55570-395-0. Index. Appendix. **VOYA** June 2001.

Focusing on public libraries and one school's media center, these enriching and readable essays present expert opinions on Internet policy and practice surrounding controversial Internet content. Many chapters repeat key phrases such as "protect the First Amendment rights," "seek community input," "filtering software is seriously flawed," and "educate parents." The bottom line in almost every section is finding the balance between the professional stance and the reality of a community. The coverage, however, is comprehensive. The American Library Association's position and legalities involving individual rights are stated clearly without the media's taint. Particularly interesting are the articles from unique perspectives or with original angles. Gordon Conable's chapter, "Dealing with Trustees," is a surprisingly fascinating glimpse into what one enlightened board member would tell others about sensible Internet policy making. Patricia Glass-Schuman's contribution clearly states the dos and don'ts of talking with the media about this contentious issue—a scary prospective for most librarians. The essays regarding establishing community websites through the library, training staff to be "on the same page," and educating parents and children with extensive Internet training are stellar best-practice models. All the authors have impressive credentials; they know their stuff and tell their stories well.

If read cover to cover, this illuminating book will expand readers' knowledge of and beliefs about the Internet content controversy. Any reader reader—frustrated parent to "library computer guy"—will come away with a fresh perspective on this issue that has no easy answers.—Elaine McGuire.

Martin, Hillias J., and James R. Murdock. **Serving Lesbian, Gay, Bisexual, Transgender, and Questioning Teens: A How-to-Do-It Manual for Librarians**. Neal-Schuman, 2007. 267p. $55 Trade pb. 978-1-55570-566-4. **VOYA** August 2007.

How should librarians serve lesbian, gay, bisexual, transgender, transsexual, and questioning youth? What if the library is located in the midst of a very conservative or rural area? What about school libraries? This manual answers these questions with clear-eyed views on the subjects of resistance to change and the needs of young adults. The authors divide the book into two main parts: Serving LGBTQ Teens in the Library is a narrative portion that touches on subjects including understanding the community, identifying information needs, providing safe spaces, building a collection, and integrating LGBTQ themes into "everyday" services like booktalks and programs. This part also contains an incredibly useful chapter called "Finding and Implementing the Right Pace for Change." Using a traffic-light analogy, the authors explain how someone in a conservative area can move at "speed 1-red light" and how a library in a city like Portland, Oregon, or Atlanta, Georgia, can move much more quickly. There is a special section for school libraries that should be useful to those who think, "But my administrator!" or "But the parents!"

The second portion of the book includes a variety of resources for librarians and teachers. It offers the "essential core collection," material lists by topic, compelling booktalks (especially useful for those who find booktalks challenging to compose and frightening to deliver on this topic), and LGBTQ programs with step-by-step instructions. The book is unusually thorough and contains many useful suggestions as well as the important and emotionally satisfying acknowledgment both of youth and librarian needs and realities. One odd omission occurs in a list of magazine resources where the authors fail to mention Curve, a lesbian magazine with national circulation. The number of books published each year with lesbian or gay youth as protagonists continues to rise although the authors note, quite rightly (and as a necessary spur to YA writers), that novels with bisexual protagonists are few and infrequently published. Only two books-Julie Anne Peters' **Luna** (Megan Tingley Books/Little, Brown, 2004/ **VOYA** June 2006) and **Parrotfish** by Ellen Wittlinger (Simon & Schuster, 2007/ **VOYA** review this issue)-focus on transsexual characters.

Every library should have this book. Following its recommendations can help branch and rural librarians justify new titles and help all librarians more fully serve the variety of young adults who enter their doors. The authors make clear that a library safe haven can do more than get reading material to young people; it can save self-esteem and in some cases, lives.—Suzi Steffen.

Mediavilla, Cindy. **Creating the Full-Service Homework Center in Your Library**. ALA Editions, 2001. 120p. Trade pb. 978-0-8389-0800-6. O.P. Index. Biblio. Appendix. **VOYA** August 2001.

The topic of how to develop an after-school homework center in a library is discussed often among librarians, and Mediavilla answers questions that anyone interested in starting this process might have. Her useful book came about after the author received an award to study homework assistance programs throughout the country. It stems from the ideas that homework centers are created to solve the unattended children problems in libraries; boost grades, test scores, and self-esteem; offer an after-school alternative; foster safety for children; and meet the goals of library mission statements. Many suggestions are provided on how to recruit and train volunteers, obtain funding, and organize or improve a program. Most of the same studies were of larger institutions with several branches or those with ample staff, resources, space, or outside funding. The difficulties of a smaller library might need to be considered further. Following the chapter are sample volunteer and student applications, job descriptions, promotional flyers, evaluation forms, and other useful ideas to get a homework center started.

There are no other books available solely on this topic, and this resource is surely definitive. Mediavilla's work will inspire librarians already developing a homework center, those who want to make theirs better, and those who never previously considered a homework center.—Jennifer Bromann.

Miller, Donna P. **Crash Course in Teen Services**. Libraries Unlimited, 2008. 128p. $30 Trade pb. 978-1-59158-565-7. Index. Biblio. **VOYA** June 2008.

Drawing on her experience as a librarian in both schools and public libraries, Miller provides sound guidance for new young adult librarians with little or no professional training in this title for the publisher's Crash Course series. The focus is on meeting the needs of teen library users, a point emphasized by the use of the term "customer" rather than the more formal "patron" to embrace the business philosophy of customer service. With references to theories on adolescence, the book stresses the practical application of that theory through programming, readers' advisory, reference, and other library services to teens. The basics of these services are briefly but adequately covered, with helpful references to both print and Web resources for more in-depth information. For example, the chapter on programming provides a basic overview of how to plan, execute, and evaluate teen programs, with a sampling of popular program ideas. This section also includes resources for brainstorming and planning additional programs, such as the Holiday Insights Web site (*http://www.holidayinsights.com*) for event-based programming. The chapter on readers' advisory likewise discusses basic formats and types of reading materials teens prefer as well as characteristics of common fiction genres and a few representative authors.

Although not as all-inclusive as Patrick Jones's **Connecting Young Adults and Libraries** (Neal-Schuman, 2004/ **VOYA** February 2005), this resource certainly provides quick and useful information to new librarians and staff working with teens, and it is especially helpful to those working in smaller public libraries, where resources and funding is often limited. The book may also be useful for providing an administrator with a quick overview of the requirements and benefits of a teen program. The down-to-earth manner and sensible approach make this book widely accessible.-Heather Christiansen.

Mueller, Jon. **Assessing Critical Skills**. Linworth, 2008. 144p. $44.95 Trade pb. 978-158683-282-7. Index. Charts. Biblio. **VOYA** April 2009.

The weakest link in the inclusion of critical skills in the curriculum has been assessment. These skills that are so necessary for the workplace and personal life include problem solving, critical thinking, and self-assessment, as well as locating, evaluating, and communicating information. Assessing these skills, however, requires different instruments from the traditional test. This professional book is a toolkit for the educator who is willing to incorporate critical skills into instruction, but who needs assistance in creating authentic assessments or is looking for new ideas in testing instruments. An explanation of authentic assessments is followed by steps in the development of instruments for evaluation of skill development. Formative and summative assessments are given for each scenario. Rubrics for rating performance for a variety of tasks across the curriculum are a key part of the book. These rubrics include solo audition, evaluation of research claims, paragraph task, and analyzing group collaboration. One chapter focuses on assessing the ability to monitor one's progress and performance, while other chapters focus on measuring information literacy skills and collaborative skills.

Educators who are familiar with current research in curriculum development and assessment will recognize many names in the extensive list of references. It will be a very valuable professional resource for any library serving educators. Classroom teachers and curriculum developers will probably want their personal copies as well.—Marilyn Brien.

Neiberger, Eli. **Gamers . . . in the Library? The Why, What, and How of Videogame Tournaments for All Ages**. ALA Editions, 2007. 190p. $50 Trade pb. 978-0-8389-0944-7. Index. Illus. Further Reading. **VOYA** February 2008.

This thin book is packed with a comprehensive plan for library staff interested in conducting console video game programs for customers of all ages, with a particular focus on teens. The quick read will cover all the necessary aspects of introducing gaming to your organization and expanding the program as appropriate. Neiburger's humor is well placed and breaks up the information to recapture attention and reflect his knowledge of how libraries and library cultures work. As the IT Manager at the Ann Arbor District Library, Neiberger creates a credible and interesting book on gaming, presenting all the practical aspects of running gaming programs and tournaments. For larger organizations, it can be passed around to appropriate teen services staff to be read quickly, and passages can help librarians discuss gaming with IT staff and administration. Chapter headlines and subcategory titles are designed to show readers the thoughtful sequence of topics through which they are progressing, and the resources at the end are on target for further reading.

This resource has a one-size-fits-all quality appropriate both for staff who have never run a gaming program and for those who might already be offering gaming in some form but want to raise the bar, expand, and keep it all organized. With the writing as vibrant as its topic, it is a must-have professional tool.-Julie Scordato.

Odden, Allan R. **Improving Student Learning When Budgets Are Tight**. Corwin, 2012. 208p. $36.95 Oversize pb. 978-1-4522-1708-6. **VOYA** August 2012.

In the current economic climate, states and school districts are cutting education budgets throughout the United States. Without a more effective use of reduced dollars and a re-examination of educational priorities, student performance—as well as the entire educational infrastructure—is at risk. Veteran educator and school reform expert Odden provides a comprehensive handbook for teachers, school administrators, and concerned citizens outlining a school improvement action plan focused on student learning. Moving beyond vague theory, Odden delivers concrete, specific suggestions that schools and districts can implement immediately to improve student learning, recruit top teachers, provide ongoing professional development, and utilize new and existing educational technologies. Six well-organized chapters make admirable use of charts, tables, and bullet points. Using case studies of actual schools in thirty-five states from Maryland to California, the author shows how using his plan of action has repeatedly optimized student learning by making effective use of reduced education budgets. Even for schools faced with devastating budget reductions, Odden always advocates retaining professional librarian positions as essential for all high-performing schools.

In lucid and jargon-free prose, the author distills the results of a lifetime of teaching, research, and educational consulting into a shrewd and workable plan to help educators move from frustration to action. His work is highly recommended for both media center professional collections and academic libraries.—Jamie Hansen.

Pearlmutter, Jane, and Paul Nelson. **Small Public Library Management**. American Library Association, 2011. 152p. $50. Oversize pb. 978-0-8389-1085-6. **VOYA** April 2012.

Managers of small public libraries do it all, but they do not necessarily know it all. This makes this title essential for library management because it provides a starting place for common administrative issues and questions. The authors, both experienced in public library leadership and affiliated with the University of Wisconsin-Madison, breakdown this handbook into "Who Do You Work For," "Library Finances," "Personnel Management," "Facilities," "Collection Management," "Services and Programs," and "The Library as Place." Although this title contains very few images, the chapters present the information in a readable format with charts, tables, and examples, which include field experience and usable checklists and forms. The topics covered are easily searchable through a detailed table of contents and thorough index.

This title, or more accurately termed a director's user manual, should be kept in close proximity to every librarian's desk in a small public library. Librarians will find value in reading this book cover to cover, as well referencing it for specific situations. Despite the slenderness of the book, the authors pack loads of information into every page. The chapter about finances is especially informative in regards to the funding practices of small libraries. Government allocations are discussed, in addition to formulas that guide collection development. Keep in mind, each topic does not go into extreme depth, but they are descriptive enough to lead the reader in the right direction. This book is definitely recommended for librarians in small public libraries.—Shanna Swigert Smith.

Perlstein, Linda. **Not Much Just Chillin': The Hidden Lives of Middle Schoolers**. Farrar Straus Giroux, 2003. 261p. 978-0-374-20882-0. O. P. Biblio. Source Notes. **VOYA** April 2004.

This anthropological study of middle schoolers is fascinating and informative. Perlstein, a reporter embedded in a suburban Columbia, Maryland, middle school, chronicles a year in the life of several "tweens"-youth who are barely teens but no longer children. Much like A Tribe Apart by Patricia Hersch (Ballantine 1998/**VOYA**, *The View from VOYA*, **VOYA** August 1998), this study digs into the hearts and minds of youth. Especially valuable for librarians and parents is the information about how life changes for this age group once it leaves elementary school behind. Not only are their bodies changing, but also their social lives and academic demands alter. The book is divided by season, beginning with autumn, and as time progresses, the author illustrates how middle schoolers quickly lose their innocence and inhibitions. An intriguing aspect of the study is how middle schoolers use instant messaging to communicate with each other. Chapter two, "Everyone Else Thinks It's a Stupid Plane Crash," describes the apathy and fear felt by students during the terrorist attacks on September 11. Whereas the teachers attempt to explain the significance of the day, some middle schoolers simply see it as a day when they got to leave school early. The author intersperses information about adolescent development with observations of students.

The book will be valuable to youth service workers and parents who want to learn more about the significant changes faced by teens when they enter middle school. It is highly recommended for public libraries, school libraries, and current and future young adult librarians.-Sheila B. Anderson.

Pierce, Jennifer Burek. **Sex, Brains, and Video Games: A Librarian's Guide to Teens in the Twenty-First Century**. ALA Editions, 2007. 162p. $42 Trade pb. 978-0-8389-0951-5. Index. Source Notes. Further Reading. **VOYA** December 2007.

The average public librarian works with teens on a daily basis, but it does not necessarily mean that they know how to properly serve that age group. Pierce tries to dispel many myths on how to work with teens in the twenty-first century. The book is broken up into several topics, the first of which explores the teen brain. There has been much research in recent years on how the brain develops, and knowing this information might help librarians to better understand teens. The other sections discuss technology, sex, and multicultural diversity with teens and libraries.

The author provides an overview of each topic along with excerpts from leading experts in the field of teens and libraries. The technology section provides great statistics about teens and usage, as well as how teens are influenced by video games, which is very helpful information for teen programmers and how they can focus on working video games into their programming. At the end of each chapter, Peirce gives an in-depth list of further reading that includes websites, along with detailed notes. The book is a good reference for teen librarians but an even better guide to potential library students who will soon be entering the field.—Robyn Guedel.

Plumb, Daria. **Commando Classics: A Field Guide for Helping Students Understand (and Maybe Even Enjoy) Classic Literature**. VOYA Press, 2012. 300p. $50. Trade pb. 978-1-61751-008-3.

**Commando Classics: A Field Guide for Helping Students Understand (and Maybe Even Enjoy) Classic Literature** was not reviewed by **VOYA**.

Polanka, Sue, Ed. **No Shelf Required 2: Use and Management of Electronic Books**. American Library Association, 2012. 272p. $65 Oversize pb. 978-0-8389-1145-7. **VOYA** June 2012.

Electronic books and their devices have the potential to offer great possibilities, but as equipment and systems are not always compatible with new advancements, those same possibilities can lead to frustration. Polanka compiled a collection of articles covering such essential information as the difference between publishing formats, the potential of enhanced electronic books, and equity of accessibility. Articles also cover issues to be considered when deciding when or how a library may incorporate electronic books or devices into its collection. The big picture is shared, but some of the articles look at specific libraries and their journeys in the electronic book world so that readers may learn from successes and struggles of those experts willing to share their experience.

**No Shelf Required 2: Use and Management of Electronic Books** follows an equally exceptional **No Shelf Required: E-Books in Libraries**. Polanka's expertise is evident, as she also writes an award-winning blog covering issues surrounding electronic books, as well as an ongoing article featured in *Booklist*, "Off the Shelf." For readers not fluent in the lingo and acronyms of the digital library world, authors of articles take time to define but quickly move on, keeping the interest of all. This is an invaluable read for anyone in the library or involved in library decision making.—Dianna Geers.

Puckett, Jason. **Zotero: A Guide for Librarians, Researchers and Educators**. American Library Association, 2011. 172p. $36 Oversize pb. 978-0-8389-8589-2. **VOYA** February 2012.

This title offers an in-depth look into the free, open-source reference management software Zotero. Created by the Center for History and New Media at George Mason University, Zotero is a research tool that helps users create and manage reference citations, archive web pages, and create and share bibliographies. This step-by-step guide provides readers with information about installing and using the software, as well as teaching the program to students and faculty. Throughout the book, the author uses examples of his own experiences working with Zotero, as well as scenarios using four fictional personas—undergraduate student, graduate student, faculty member, and academic librarian—helping to give the reader a better understanding of Zotero's uses.

The author provides detailed information about the software, incorporating helpful examples and practical tips in each chapter. **Zotero: A Guide for Librarians, Researchers, and Educators** is written clearly and concisely, making the reference management software easy to understand by limiting technical jargon. Although written for educators and librarians involved in higher education, **Zotero** may have a place in high school and public libraries using reference management software, teaching research skills, or preparing students for college. In these cases, this book is highly recommended, as it provides great ideas for using Zotero in a library setting.—Stacy Holbrook.

**Reaching Out to Religious Youth: A Guide to Services, Programs, and Collections**. L. Kay Carman and Carol S. Reich, Eds. Libraries Unlimited, 2004. 222p. $42 Trade pb. 978-0-313-32041-5. Biblio. **VOYA** April 2005.

Public young adult librarians have long needed this invaluable resource. Taking a broader stance than recent religious bibliographies, such as John Mort's Christian Fiction: A Guide to the Genre (Libraries Unlimited, 2002/ **VOYA** June 2003) and Barbara J. Walker's Developing Christian Fiction Collections for Children and Adults (Neal-Schumann, 1998/ **VOYA** December 1998), this book covers materials and services not only for Evangelical and mainline Protestant teens (and makes a useful distinction between them), but also focuses in equal depth on Roman Catholics, Latter-day Saints, Orthodox Christians, Seventh-Day Adventists, Jews, Muslims, Buddhists, and Hindus. Each chapter is written, if possible, by a person of that faith, and all are vetted by authorities in that religion. Bibliographies encompass not only print fiction and nonfiction, but also many audio, video, and Internet resources and even listservs for teens of each faith. Most print materials are from religious presses, although books from secular publishers are included when relevant. Also excellent are the clear and well-researched sections on the history, beliefs, and practices of each religion, as well as careful examinations of misconceptions and stereotypes (the section on Islam is particularly good in this regard).

These fascinating comparative religion sections can be used with confidence by teens for reports or personal inquiry. Each section also gives insights into a particular religious teen population with a description of formative experiences, suggestions of what those young adults might want from the library, and programming ideas. Full of nifty tips such as which Christian teen not to have on the advisory council and what foods are okay for Muslim or Hindu library gatherings, this book should be on the desk of every YA librarian.-Patty Campbell, Guest Reviewer.

## Reflective Teaching, Reflective Learning: How to Develop Critically Engaged Readers, Writers, and Speakers. Thomas M. McCann, et al., Eds. Heinemann, 2005. 223p. $35 Trade pb. 978-0-325-00852-3. **VOYA** April 2006.

It has been a while since a single book has so powerfully changed this reviewer's thinking about teaching, making her reconsider how she teaches. The book at first seems a bit of a "love fest" among the editors as it is founded on the principles presented by George Hillocks's Teaching Writing as a Reflective Practice (Teacher's College Press, 1995). The editors frequently mention his work and influence as well as each other. Readers will get over this reaction as soon as they recognize the valuable insights on teaching and learning. Interest will peak in Chapter 2 where Markham claims "education is essentially an ethical endeavor." The next chapter solidifies interest by offering an idea that teachers will immediately want to use; Flanagan presents a game to teach students the elements of an argument to enhance their writings. But it was repeated references to what Csikszentmihalyi and Larson describe as "the flow of academic experiences" that truly change perspectives. Smith offers suggestions for using student's "literate activities outside of school" to give control and competence back to students so that they might in fact enjoy what they do at school.

This book offers a wealth of practical teaching and learning activities founded on sound research. Each chapter starts with the author's reflection on a teaching practice and offers solutions to problems. Almost every chapter models Hillocks's "instructional scaffolding," and they are grouped into inquiry, writing, discussion, and literature instruction. Recommend this book to both novice and veteran teachers, as suggested in the introduction, "as a means for initiating dialogue with their peers about how to teach English."-Ann T. Reddy-Damon.

Reichman, Henry. **Censorship and Selection: Issues and Answers for Schools**. 3rd Ed. ALA Editions, 2001. 223p. $50. Trade pb. 978-0-8389-0798-6. Index. Biblio. Source Notes. Further Reading. Appendix. **VOYA** October 2001.

With challenges to both public and school library materials on the rise, Reichman's manual provides sound practical advice on how to handle this complex and emotionally charged subject. Updated to include extensive information on Internet filtering, the third edition also highlights challenges to gay and lesbian literature, witchcraft, and the occult—all potentially controversial topics. Citing statistics from several studies that provide theoretical groundwork, Reichman examines the complexion of the censor, both in terms of motivation (family values, political views, religion, and minority rights) and personality. He reviews the wide range of issues in dispute, from so-called dirty words and sex education to violence and secular humanism. The author stresses the importance of establishing sound selection policies that are crafted carefully and are administered consistently. Recommendations for handling complaints and requests for reconsideration are illustrated with school-specific examples. A chapter on law and censorship specific to school and public libraries offers a concise but comprehensive overview of how the legal system views First Amendment rights within the field of public education.

Reichman admirably balances disdain for the act of censorship with respect for the right of an individual to have a forum for voicing personal beliefs and concerns. The appendixes are especially helpful and include a school system checklist, a workbook for selection policy writing, a sample policy, and summaries of selected legal cases. Unfortunately, the bibliography is somewhat dated, covering the past decade rather than concentrating on more recent publications. Along with Ann Symon's **Protecting the Right to Read** (Neal-Schumann, 1995/**VOYA** June 1996), Reichman's book should be required reading for all school media specialists and public librarians.—Cindy Lombardo.

Schall, Lucy. **Teen Genre Connections: From Booktalking to Booklearning**. Libraries Unlimited, 2005. 318p. $42 Trade pb. 978-1-59158-229-8. Index. **VOYA** June 2006.

Help is here for harried young adult librarians, media specialists, teachers, and teen group leaders. Schall provides a useful and well-organized compendium of background information, booktalks, and activities for more than one hundred YA titles. Happily most of these books are recently published. The author also includes graphic novels and nonfiction titles, often ignored in such works, as well as suggested reading/interest levels and related works. This resource is divided into broad sections with captions like "Issues," "Contemporary Life," "Fantasy/Science Fiction/Paranormal," and "Multiple Cultures." Under "Multiple Cultures," for example, Schall offers three subdivisions, "Mixed Cultures," "World Cultures," and "Multi-Cultural America." The first includes titles such as Mildred Taylor's The Land and Richard Mosher's Zazoo, whereas the second offers works such as Thursday's Child by Sonya Hartnett and Linda Sue Park's Newbery winner, A Single Shard. Finally "Multi-Cultural America" includes Money Hungry and Begging for Change by Sharon G. Flake and Born Confused by Tanuja Desai Hidier.

Schall's booktalks are models of their kind-brief, tantalizing, and right on target for young adult listeners. Her "Learning Opportunities" (follow-up activities) are generally excellent, ranging from simple to challenging, and include writing and viewing projects, group activities, and class discussions. Practical, clearly written, and admirably planned, this title should be a required purchase for the professional collections of all those serving young adults. Jamie S. Hansen.

Scheeren, William O. **Technology for the School Librarian: Theory and Practice**. ABC-CLIO, 2010. 161p. $50. Trade pb. 978-1-59158-900-6. **VOYA** June 2010.

**Technology for the School Librarian** is a user-friendly book for the seasoned and future school librarian, the educator, and the school team, including administrators and parents. Technology in our schools is crucial, and all stakeholders need to understand its relevance in today's world. In the words of Scheeren, "While books are still at the heart of the library, technology has become the circulatory system without which that heart would not beat." Hence not only the importance of technology in the school library but also the implementation of technology, as well as the day-to-day workings of the school library, are addressed in this well-written, easy-to-read and understand manual. The author introduces important technological terms and concepts in each chapter while defining them in a clear, well-organized manner. Chapters on integrating technology into the classroom and technology for inclusion are good resources for educators with actual Web sites and ideas that can be implemented immediately in the classroom. The questions for research and discussion at the end of each chapter are valuable not only to the reader but also to schools creating mission statements, school improvement plans, or working documents. This book covers it all, from the role of school librarians, networks, and hardware and software for school libraries to technology for the twenty-first century and beyond. This is a must read and a wonderful resource for all schools.—Lona Trulove.

Schoenberg, Ruth, et al. **Reading for Understanding: A Guide to Improving Reading in Middle and High School Classrooms**. Jossey-Bass, 1999. 240p. $30 Trade pb. 978-0-7879-5045-3. Source Notes. **VOYA** August 2001.

It is rare to find a voice of such optimism regarding the possibility of dramatically improving the reading skills of students who reach the middle grades and high schools inadequately prepared to read and understand the texts required of them in all their content classes. It is also rare to find a book that focuses on improving reading skills, acknowledging the critical role of libraries, both school and public, in accomplishing this task. This professional resource does both. In it, the authors describe the Strategic Literacy Initiative, a research and professional development project based at WestEd, one of the nation's Regional Educational Laboratories. The **Guide** describes the initiative, which takes two forms. One is a reading-apprentice approach for teachers in all subject areas, and the other, using the same approach, is via a year-long course for students called Academic Literacy. Beginning with a conceptual discussion of the underpinnings of the program, the guide then provides a framework for understanding it, and continues with a description of how to implement an Academic Literacy course, complete with suggested activities. Descriptions of how teacher in the Strategic Literacy Network are embedding the approach in their regular classes and a discussion of professional development and how to establish a school-wide reading apprenticeship program complete the guide. Unfortunately, there is neither an index nor a bibliography. Source notes are provided at the end of each chapter.

For most teachers, including school library media specialists, for whom this resource is not sufficient to get them started replicating the program, WestEd provides professional development workshops. Those interested in the Initiative can find additional information on the websites at *http://www.WestEd.org* and *http://www.WestEd.org/stratlit*. This book should be a required purchase for every professional collection in middle/junior high and high schools.—Sue Rosenzweig.

**Serving Older Teens**. Sheila B. Anderson, Ed. Libraries Unlimited, 2004. 240p. $42 Trade pb. 978-0-313-31762-0. Index. Illus. Biblio. **VOYA** June 2004.

Hooray! Here is an excellent guide for serving a group of readers easily overlooked in the library community-older adolescents between the ages of sixteen and nineteen. Often preoccupied with required reading for school, while simultaneously juggling jobs, sports, and social activities, older teens can lose touch with the rhythms and tastes of their own reading selves. Librarians might be at a loss for methods to guide them, despite the fact that there are so many outstanding books throughout the collection that might serve as enticement. Like the proverbial friend in need, this resource is bursting with ideas to enhance (or create, in some instances) library services to older teen patrons. Beginning with the task of recognizing the unique needs of readers in this age group, Anderson offers statistical information that verifies their existence and psychological evidence demonstrating their developmental needs. A chapter by Patrick Jones brushes aside well-meaning constructions concerning what teens should read and gives some great insight into what they actually like to read. Amy Alessio has ideas about arranging the physical space of the library to welcome older teens, Kristine Mahood offers suggestions for booktalks, and Robyn Lupa takes readers into the YA world beyond printed material.

Best of all, this book is packed with annotated bibliographies. Any imaginable angle of classification, both fiction and nonfiction, is covered. If one loves reading and recommending literature to young adults, this book will be a nirvana! And if one finds young adults baffling and unapproachable, here is a wealth of tools to expand one's library skills when dealing with this dynamic age group.-Diane Emge.

Shamburg, Christopher. **Student-Powered Podcasting: Teaching for 21st-Century Literacy**. International Society for Technology for Education, 2009. 194p. $32.95 Trade pb. 978-1-56484-261-9. Photos. Charts. Biblio. Appendix. **VOYA** December 2009.

Introducing technology in a classroom or library environment can be challenging, especially when adult leadership feels as if their knowledge is less than the students. It can also be tricky to implement new initiatives in these settings if administration does not see value in the venture. This resource prepares educators to aid students in creating their own podcasts, provides lesson plans, and sets forth the correlation to seven sets of educational standards used throughout the country. The purpose of the text is to encourage and empower educators not only to instruct students on how to create and edit podcasts, but also to learn through podcasting. Just as writing across the curriculum has changed how students are taught, podcasting across the curriculum puts literacy as the main objective, and incorporates social processes to encourage student creativity and participation.

From defining podcast and other terms to providing instruction on using audio editing programs **Audacity** and **GarageBand** to setting forth specific objectives for varied projects including reader's theater, historical interviews, fanfiction, and many others, Shamburg's practical approach and concise information empowers the reader to implement methods in a classroom or library setting. The information is presented logically and cohesively. The charts featuring the related educational standards are especially useful for public school teachers. Copyright and fair use are addressed in the appendixes. This excellent work deftly introduces podcasting technology and tools and generates enthusiasm among young people by addressing many interests, as well as educational objectives.—Molly Krichten.

Sima, Judy, and Kevin Cordi. **Raising Voices: Creating Youth Storytelling Groups and Troupes**. Libraries Unlimited, 2003. 241p. $37 Trade pb. 978-1-56308-919-0. Index. **VOYA** February 2004.

For those teachers and librarians who believe in story and the value of storytelling with youth, this book is a must-purchase. Written by two veteran storytellers, not only does this guide provide valuable rationale about the value of storytelling for youth, but it also offers specific steps for organizing groups of young "tellers," including time-tested exercises for developing various telling skills. Throughout, the tone is consistently respectful of youth developmental needs, talents, and energy. Ways to coach and guide the youth storyteller without being heavy-handed are an integral part of the text. Beginning with initial preparation for the first meeting, chapters describe ways to teach getting ready to tell stories, learning the stories, and even creating one's own stories. A savvy and critical chapter talks about keeping the group motivated and attendance consistent, and this chapter includes a "behavior contract." The final section lists storytelling resources such as collections; single stories; sources for puppets, props, and instruments; media; Web sites; and organizations.

Sima offers a highly recommended purchase worth every penny for those seeking fun ways to program and facilitate skill-development with an age group already using stories, jokes, and gossip as ways of communicating with peers and as means to rite of passage.-Evie Wilson-Lingbloom.

Simpson, Carol. **Copyright for Administrators**. Linworth, 2008. 128p. $39.95 Trade pb. 978-1-58683-323-7. Glossary. Index. Source Notes. Appendix. **VOYA** April 2009.

School administrators who are struggling with understanding copyright as it pertains to the various types of media now available need look no further than this informative volume. In clear concise text, Simpson covers all aspects of copyright law. The chapters on computer software, Internet, and digital media are particularly informative as there is very little copyright information available for these formats. Simpson answers questions that teachers, principals and other staff are asking about topics such as public performance rights for audio visual materials and what print materials they can and cannot copy. She points out that it is essential for school administrators to be aware of copyright law, as it could end up costing them not only thousands of dollars but hours of time in court as well.

Simpson deftly handles this complex topic, making it easy for readers to quickly find the information they need rather paging through chapter after chapter of unneeded text. To further aid readers, a variety of appendixes with useful tools such as a sample copyright policy and a list of important Internet links for copyright information are included. Simpson finishes up with a glossary that even a copyright novices will have no trouble using.—Shari Fesko.

Simpson, Martha Sief, and Lucretia I. Duwel. **Bringing Classes into the Public Library: A Handbook for Librarians**. McFarland, 2007. 175p. $49.95 Trade pb. 978-0-7864-2806-9. Index. Illus. Appendix. **VOYA** December 2007.

It is an age old struggle. Children's librarians need to get classes into the public library, but what to do once the students arrive? Once librarians are finished reading this offering, however, there will be no doubt about how to pack them in and keep them. The authors offer blow-by-blow details on how to draw schools into visiting. Readers will learn about the components of successful class visits including approaching potential advocates for the library, delegating staff responsibilities, and actively engaging parents. It also helps that the authors provide programming suggestions tailored to the grade levels being served by the class visit. Clear, descriptive outlines ensure that readers will know everything to include in packets to send home with the youth both before and after their library visits. There are even reproducible handouts in the book's appendix that are sure to be both entertaining and educational for students.

Those just entering the field can use this resource as an effective tool in getting their school visits off the ground. This book is not limited to the profession's newest faces. Seasoned professionals will benefit from the book's refresher tips and new ideas. It is a highly recommended purchase for public librarians and should be one that is kept in every public library's children's room as a reference.-Robbie L. Flowers.

Singer, Paula M. and Gail Griffith. **Succession Planning in the Library: Developing Leaders, Managing Change**. American Library Association, 2010. 160p. $55. Trade pb. 978-0-8389-1036-8. **VOYA** August 2010.

Authors Singer and Griffith address the reader about succession planning, why libraries need it, and how libraries of any size can benefit from it. The authors cite many case studies in which succession planning helps identify needs and plan for the future. The case studies are laid out in an easy-to-read format, with graphs and charts that display the different approaches libraries use to identify needs.

Succession planning is useful for staff development planning, working relationships among staff, retirement issues, organizational challenges, and attracting and retaining qualified professionals for the long term.

The vision of the book is to help directors identify key issues in competencies of current employee, spotting potential leaders, professional growth and retention of employees in an ever-changing multigenerational workplace. This professional reference is a valuable tool for all library managers, directors, and trustees in developing long-term goals that address the current and future needs of their library, regardless of the size and scope of the library.—Mark Irish.

Smallwood, Carol, Ed. **Library Management Tips That Work**. American Library Association, 2011. 208p. $55 Oversize pb. 978-0-8389-1121-1. Index. Table of contents. **VOYA** February 2012.

This book offers a wealth of information for any informational professional, management or otherwise. The book is not lengthy but covers a wide array of topics that are categorized as manager's role, running a library, information technology, staff, and public relations. These categories contain chapters written by various library professionals from both public and academic libraries. Each chapter is very small, but the information is concise and examples are provided. The book is written as a manual for common issues, so readers may refer to specific chapters as needed. A detailed table of contents and thorough index are available, as well as a list of contributors with biographies. The author biographies are especially helpful in gleaning the authority of a chapter's information.

This book is pleasantly surprising; it is quick and easy to read, and there is continuity to the writing, despite the large number of authors. Additionally, pertinent and current issues are addressed, such as connecting with student employees via Facebook. It is also important to mention that this book does not necessarily need to be read straight through because the formatting allows for browsing and skimming. Librarians should familiarize themselves with the subjects covered in this book, and then keep the title close at hand for when those issues arise.—Shanna Swigert Smith.

Smallwood, Carol, Ed. **The Frugal Librarian: Thriving in Tough Economic Times**. American Library Association, 2011. 280p. $42. Trade pb. 978-0-8389-1075-7. Charts. Index. Biblio. **VOYA** June 2011.

The thirty-four chapters in Smallwood's collection address a myriad of issues faced by libraries and librarians when times get tough and money is tight. Written by practicing librarians from academic, public, and school libraries, the concise essays are easy to read, sometimes personal, and highly practical. Each chapter can stand alone, so the volume can serve as a reference tool for a librarian needing specific help; or the entire volume can be perused from start to finish. One section of essays addresses the issue of "librarian survival" in an economic down-turn and includes ideas on taking advantage of inexpensive professional development opportunities, parlaying non-traditional experience into job security, and surviving a layoff. A section on grants points librarians to a variety of revenue resources and gives pointers on writing grant proposals. Other sections cover the challenge of managing libraries with smaller (or frozen) budgets, including cancellation decisions and outreach strategies; creative approaches to staffing challenges; and novel ways to share resources, including open-source catalogs.

This issue is certainly timely, but in reality, sound management and creative budgeting never vanish from the library environment. The table of contents and descriptive title chapters, coupled with the index, allow for ease of use for the browser. This inexpensive volume from ALA will be particularly helpful to public and academic librarians.—Melissa Moore.

Smith, Michael W., and Jeffrey D. Wilhelm. **"Reading Don't Fix No Chevys": Literacy in the Lives of Young Men**. Heinemann, 2002. 248p. $33.75 Trade pb. 978-0-86709-509-8. Index. Biblio. Charts. Appendix. **VOYA** August 2002.

Smith and Wilhelm, two secondary English teachers concerned about boys' resistance to school reading tasks and their underachievement, studied the reading habits of thirty-two boys among high- to low-achieving students in four school districts. They collected four kinds of data—rankings of various literate activities and interviews about the rankings; reactions to constructed profiles of boys engaged in various literate activities and interviews about their responses; journals of everything read, written, watched, or listened to at school and at home for three months, with interviews about the journals; and observations of the boys inside and outside of class. The book profiles these young people and quotes from them extensively, making the book a model for this type of research. For practitioners, the results are significant. Smith and Wilhelm found that social networks and connections, often facilitated by computer communication, were important for reading selection. Significantly, they learned that English teachers were outside the network. Boys rejected "schoolish" forms of literacy. They expected to be engaged in the first few paragraphs, liked stories over facts, and put great importance on visual texts such as on websites, television shows, and movies. They liked reading that could be exported into conversation, including newspaper accounts, headlines, box scores, and jokes. They preferred texts that sustain engagement for repeated readings and that provide multiple perspectives. They wanted texts that were novel as opposed to routine; have edgy, subversive content and powerful ideas; and are funny. The book closes with portraits of the boys and implications for teaching.

Besides the findings of this particular study, the book is worth its price for the summary of research on boys and literacy as well as for its implications for library collections and services for male adolescents. This book is a must-read for young adult librarians.—Mary K. Chelton.

Sutton, Roger, and Martha Parravano. **A Family of Readers: The Book Lover's Guide to Children's and Young Adult Literature**. Candlewick Press, 2010. 350 p. $22. 978-0-7636-3280-9. Index. Biblio. Source Notes. **VOYA** October 2010.

This collection of essays from editors, reviewers, and authors emanates enthusiasm for books and reading. The introduction sets the stage, calling it "a book for readers, people who need books as much as food or air." Each section begins with an overview, followed by a selection of essays. The first chapter addresses the very smallest book lovers, and the last tackles the needs of young adults. Each chapter is followed by an annotated list of books. A complete bibliography and biographical sketches of the contributors are included at the end. The essays abound with wonderful quotes, underscoring how literature enriches life. Mitali Perkins quips, "I know exactly why Peter Pan flew back to Neverland." Vicky Smith, commenting on **Julie of the Wolves** (HarperTeen, 2003) says, "If Miyax could survive . . . with nothing but a needle and a couple of knives, then surely I could make it through gym class."

As a professional review journal with eighty-five years of experience, **The Hornbook Magazine** is uniquely qualified to offer expert advice on juvenile literature. Editor-in-chief of the journal, Roger Sutton, explains, "this is a book that features informed opinions from passionate readers, not bland lists of dos, don'ts and surefire recommendations." Eminently readable and often humorous, each entry speaks ardently to what children long for and need at each stage of their development. It should be required reading for every youth services librarian.—Nancy Wallace.

Taffel, Ron, with Melinda Blau. **Second Family: How Adolescent Power is Challenging the American Family**. St. Martin's, 2001. 256p. $12.95 Trade pb. 978-0-312-26137-5. **VOYA** August 2001.

Although this book is addressed to parents, the points it makes are too important for librarians, educators, and youth workers to categorize it so narrowly. Taffel, a child and family therapist, describes what he calls the second family of the adolescent peer group and the comforts—excitement, entertainment, and stimulation—it provides to adolescents. This support network goes unknown and unseen by the often time-stressed, multitasking adults in their lives, who are isolated from each other as much as from the kids in their care. He says that the old notion of the peer group is dead. Although peers still can be extremely hurtful, when a compatible group is found, it offers the psychic sustenance often lacking in adult-adolescent relationships, in part because they do not pressure each other. Parents, meanwhile, have abdicated or have trouble asserting their own authority and values. He suggests for adults a blending of empathy—being interested in kids' activities and feelings—with clear expectations and consequences, so that kids will trust them when real help is needed. Of particular interest are his chapters "You Don't Have a Clue," which describes the adolescent conspiracy of silence from adults, so complicit in recent school shootings, and "Don't Let Me Slip Away," on how kids lie because of confusion over right and wrong.

It is not that Taffel covers new ground here. He just manages to explain a bewildering array of adolescent behaviors and social phenomena in a new way. Of particular importance are his suggestions for adult networks to help kids. School and public young adult librarians should be part of them, and his book is required reading for anyone interacting with adolescents today. It is a particularly fascinating follow-up to James Garbarino's **Lost Boys** (The Free Press, 1999/**VOYA** December 1999).—Mary K. Chelton.

Taylor, Joie. **Information Literacy and the School Library Media Center**. Libraries Unlimited, 2006. 149p. $37 Trade pb. 978-0-313-32020-0. Index. Illus. Biblio. **VOYA** August 2006.

Taylor recognizes that at the heart of the library media program is the need to educate students to be informed and savvy users of information. Nobody is better equipped to guide students to information literacy competence than the library media specialist, and Taylor's book is a thorough and well-researched guide to how they can accomplish this task. Beginning with a description of what it means to be information literate, the author goes on to highlight how the American Association of School Librarians (AASL) and Association for Educational Communications and Technology (AECT) standards can be integrated into the curriculum in ways that complement state and district standards, giving specific examples from several states. She discusses how the library media specialist through flexible scheduling and curriculum mapping can facilitate an environment where students can hone their information literacy skills. Taylor advocates that students learn a research process and highlights the similarities between several recognized research models. She not only provides examples of different ways research results can be modeled, she also suggests several ideas for assessing these activities to make sure those students have mastered research skills successfully.

Two things make this book exceptional. First the chapter on collaboration is a refreshingly frank discussion of the value of working with classroom teachers that delineates the roles of the teacher and the library media specialist, while being realistic in realizing that barriers do exist to real collaboration. Second the extensive bibliography is filled with books, journal articles, and Web resources that will guide readers to the best practices in information literacy at the current time.-Chris Carlson.

**Teaching Generation M: A Handbook for Librarians and Educators**. Neal-Schuman Publishers, 2009. Vibiana Bowman Cvetkovic and Robert J. Lackie, Eds. 368p. $85. 978-1-55570-667-8. Index. Illus. Biblio. **VOYA** December 2009.

Great for librarians and teachers who work with young adults, this professional handbook tackles three important topics—who is the millennial generation, what kind of world do millennials live in, and what can we do to teach them? Chapter topics include media literacy, the information search process, **Facebook, YouTube, Google**, and **Wikipedia**, gaming, webcomics, mobile technology, cooperative learning, screencasting, and the new generation of research papers. Do you need to protect your library's **Facebook** fan page? Cite this book. Do you need to defend why YouTube should not be filtered in your school library? Consult this book.

Each chapter is written by a different person and extensive lists of references, both online and print, are included. The contributors are mainly university library professors, providing research-based essays on their topic. Most references are from the past five years, and some chapters have very useful lists of recommended readings and resources. In-text citations make this book more of a resource than a pleasure read, but it is a must-read for non-M-generation librarians new to young adult services and for those new teachers or anyone wanting to understand Web 2.0.—Sarah Hill.

Toor, Ruth, and Hilda K. Weisburg. **Being Indispensable: A School Librarian's Guide to Becoming an Invaluable Leader**. ALA, 2010. 184p. $42. Trade pb. 978-0-8389-1065. Index. Source notes. Appendix. **VOYA** April 2011.

Most school librarians will tell you: we have the best job in the world. Unfortunately, in these tough economic times, keeping that job and maintaining exemplary library programs can be challenging. It is the rare school librarian who is not concerned about the impact of shrinking budgets. A book that offers to help us establish ourselves as indispensable in our buildings could not be more welcome—particularly when it delivers on its promise as well as this one. Written by two recently retired school librarians with decades of experience and years of leadership roles at the national and regional levels, this is a practical, comprehensive guide filled with recommendations and suggestions that are firmly grounded in reality.

Every piece of advice in this book—whether it is planning an "elevator talk," defining a mission, managing time, or developing a strategic plan—is designed to help school librarians demonstrate their critical importance to the school's educational program. The authors offer concrete suggestions for understanding and addressing the wants and needs of all library stakeholders, whether they be first-graders or local business leaders. Chapters are brief, and include exercises for reader response and reflection. Each section includes thoughtful discussion questions, and a summary of key ideas. An annotated list of Web resources provides further help and information. This is an excellent book to share with a Professional Learning Community of school librarians. It is sure to be a useful resource for personal enrichment and professional development.—Jane Harper.

Trotta, Marcia. **Staff Development on a Shoestring: A How-To-Do-It Manual for Librarians**. Neal-Schuman, 2011. 176p. $65. Oversize pb. 978-1-55570-730-9. Index. Appendix. Charts. **VOYA** June 2011.

Chapter by chapter, Trotta walks a staff development coordinator through all phases of a successful staff development program. The author begins by making the case for training from within and developing a core group of staff development trainers, as limited funds make bringing in outside speakers cost prohibitive. Trotta then turns the reader's attention to the macro level of staff development—the goal planning and vision making. With limited budgets, library directors must make sure their staff development programs address specific needs in their libraries. Examples of on-going staff development programs are given. Before turning outside your library, Trotta discusses the benefits of an in-house mentoring program. In looking outside your library for low-cost or free staff development programs, Trotta explores several e-learning avenues. The author ends by delving into the need for effective staff development evaluation and provides resources for further study.

**Staff Development on a Shoestring** is rich with planning sheets, example questionnaires, and even topics to include in a successful staff development program. Trotta has a firm grasp of the topic, as the retired director of the Meriden, Connecticut, public libraries, and as author of previous books on library management and staff development for this publisher. The volume provides a wealth of information for managers of large libraries, both public and private. With library budgets being cut nationwide, this volume would be a handy reference for staff development coordinators at large library systems.—Charla Hollingsworth.

Tuccillo, Diane P. **Library Teen Advisory Groups**. **VOYA** Books/Scarecrow Press, 2004. 165p. $29.95 Trade pb. 978-0-8108-4982-2. Index. Illus. Photos. Biblio. Appendix. **VOYA** February 2005.

> **Library Teen Advisory Groups** was not reviewed by **VOYA**, which was also published by Scarecrow Press at the time of the book's publication.

Tuccillo, Diane P. **Teen-Centered Library Service: Putting Youth Participation into Practice**. Libraries Unlimited, 2010. 259p. $45. 978-1-59158-765-1. Biblio. Further Reading. **VOYA** August 2010.

> If your library wants proof of how teen participation enhances library services look no further than Diane P. Tuccillo's **Teen-Centered Library Service**. Tuccillo expands upon workshops she developed to deliver a comprehensive look at how teen-centered services support teens' emotional and brain development, promote "resiliency," and enable libraries to forge partnerships and collaborations that serve users of all ages. With examples from specific school and public libraries, chapter end notes and further readings, **Teen-Centered Library Service** is a hands-on resource that not only tells librarians why teen participation matters, it also shows them how to achieve it.

> Like other teen-focused professional resources, Tuccillo's book includes background information about teen development and the Search Institute's Developmental Assets. Beyond that are six chapters that focus on how to initiate teen participation in areas such as: advisory boards and volunteering, interactive programming (writing contests, poetry slams), temporary involvement (service days), technology (Web site maintenance), community outreach (school partnerships), and contributing to adult groups (friends and trustees). Concluding the work are chapters that provide ideas about keeping teens involved, training them and evaluating teen participation. Within each chapter are forms, flyers and contacts that allow readers to further explore how they might best incorporate teens into programs and planning.

> In the end, this book serves as a clearinghouse of teen participation research, as well as a "how to" manual. **Teen-Centered Library Service** is a must-have resource for libraries still new to teen participation, as well as those looking to invigorate tired programs.—Jessica Appel.

**Using Literature to Help Troubled Teens Cope with Abuse Issues**. Joan Kaywell, Ed. Greenwood, 2004. PLB $49.95. 978-0-313-30715-7. Index. **VOYA** April 2005.

> Last but definitely not least, the final addition to the Using Literature to Help Troubled Teens series is a well-written book. Prior books in the series focus on issues relating to family, society, alienation and identity, health, and end-of-life. The editor is a professor of English Education and the contributors are counselors, educators, social workers, librarians, and a behavioral specialist. The book is divided into four parts: Neglect,

Emotional Abuse, Physical Abuse, and Sexual Abuse. Each part gives a definition of the type of abuse, statistics, results of the abuse, how to recognize abused teens, and young adult novels related to the type of abuse being discussed. Each chapter discusses ways to help abused teens through the use of popular young adult literature, including books by Margaret Peterson Haddix, Heather Quarles, Chris Crutcher, Han Nolan, James Deem, Laurie Halse Anderson, Jacqueline Woodson, and Beatrice Sparks. For each entry, the contributors provide an introduction to and a synopsis of the book, as well as responses to the story from readers, counselors, and therapists.

Anyone interested in realistic teen literature or bibliotherapy will love this thorough dissection of books about teen abuse. It is highly recommended for parents, counselors, school libraries, and public libraries.-Sheila B. Anderson.

Vaillancourt, Renee J. **Bare Bones Young Adult Services: Tips for Public Library Generalists**. ALA Editions, 1999. 120p. $40 Trade pb. 978-0-8389-3497-5. Index. Appendix. Source Notes. Charts. **VOYA** August 2000.

This manual belongs on the professional of every library—whether or not it has a young adult department or young adult librarian. It also should be available at every university offering a graduate degree in library science. It is the most basic, affordable guide on how to set up, expand, and/or improve library services to teens. It includes chapters on the philosophy of young adult services and youth participation, on creating a space in libraries for young adults, on collection development, and on teen services that libraries should offer. The author discusses intellectual freedom, behavior issues and strategies, and continuing education for YA librarians. The many appendixes include the Young Adult Library Services Association (YALSA) Competencies for Libraries Serving Youth, tips on evaluating YA literature and websites, how to write and present a booktalk to groups, information literacy standards for student learning, a sample YA program evaluation, the Library Bill of Rights, and The Freedom t Read Statement.

Vaillancourt, assistant director for the Missoula Public Library in Montana and long time member of YALSA, has done an excellent job of balancing the philosophy of services to young adults with practical how-to suggestions. This is an excellent read for brand new teen librarians or experienced librarians switching to the young adult field. Experienced YA librarians also should reread this informative text occasionally to ensure that their program stays fresh and their focus is on target. With this manual available in every library, there really is no excuse for poor—or worse—absent service to teens.--Debby Adams.

Valenza, Joyce Kasman. **Power Research Tools: Learning Activities and Posters**. ALA Editions, 2003. 114p. pb $64. 978-0-8389-0838-9. Charts. Posters. Lesson Organizers. **VOYA** October 2003.

Valenza takes Information Power's information literacy standards (ALA, 1998/ **VOYA** August 1999) and turns them into actual lessons that teach real-life, information-seeking skills to youth drowning in information. The book is a follow up to her earlier Power Tools (ALA, 1998) and serves as a guide to more meaningful research activities for students. Developed in collaboration with other faculty at Springfield Township High

School in Pennsylvania, Valenza's work presents four sections on searching for information, ethics, evaluation of information, and organizing and communicating information. Each section starts with the standards being addressed, identifies the related posters from those that come with the book, and gives activities and handouts, with organizers and instructions for students. Examples for practice are teen centered, such as those for selecting the right search engine: "Is there a risk of carpal tunnel syndrome for young people who play video games excessively?" or "Are school cliques harmful to teenage girls?" Of particular value is a page for teachers on how to discourage plagiarism, suggesting strategies such as requiring students to submit all drafts and outlines along with the final project and requiring an annotated bibliography. Citation styles, documentation versus plagiarism, and how to weave quotes into original writing are also included. The chapter on evaluation of sources uses a poster displaying an acronym, CARRDSS, for credibility, accuracy, reliability, relevance, date, sources behind the text, and scope, with several reflection exercises on the process and a rubric for assessing the student's search process. The organizing section is equally meticulous.

This book is superb for anyone trying to break down the pieces of the information search process into meaningful, interesting lessons for students. The posters that come with it should be displayed near the computers in any library offering Internet access for any age, especially "The Free Web is Not Enough" and "What's Not on the Free Web?" as well as the three on Boolean operators and "Search Engines Essentials." Valenza's manual is a mandatory purchase for secondary school library media specialists, public reference, young adult librarians, and library school instructors teaching reference and information literacy instruction.-Mary K. Chelton.

Welch, Rollie James. **The Guy-Friendly YA Library: Serving Male Teens**. Libraries Unlimited, 2007. 196p. $40 Trade pb. 978-1-59158-270-0. Index. **VOYA** October 2007.

This professional resource covers much ground in its eight chapters. With the premise that young males are underserved in many libraries, Welch, the Teen Coordinator of the Cleveland Public Library System, lays out a blueprint that he hopes will make administrators, librarians, and teachers more aware of the needs of teen boys. A discussion of three components to serve this demographic is included. Those three components are having a full-time designated teen librarian, promotion of materials for these teens, and knowing the needs of young adult males. Chapters three through five make up the heart of the book and give detailed information on male reading habits, reluctant readers, topics of interest for boys, and many novel recommendations-some common, others more obscure-from several different genres. The role of the librarian in how to engage teens and how to connect with teens both in the library and with school visits is also included. Welch is also a realist and understands that programming, budget, and politics can also cause havoc on some recommendations.

If reaching more teen males is a goal, this wonderful and highly readable resource to making libraries more guy-friendly is an excellent place to start. The book is short and not meant to be all-inclusive. Many short lists of recommended books for guys-"The Quick 5"-are sprinkled throughout the text. These lists cover many different types of literature including various genres of nonfiction and fiction. Although the title of the book is straightforward and librarians are clearly the audience, teachers might miss out or steer clear of this book because the title contains the term "library." Teachers would be well served to peruse this well-organized and insightful introduction.-Jeff Mann.

**Why We Teach**. Sonia Nieto, Ed. Teachers College Press, 2005. 242p. $21.95 Trade pb. 978-0-8077-4593-9. Index. Photos. Notes. Further Reading. **VOYA** October 2006.

This collection of essays written by teachers across the country demonstrates exactly why there is hope for our public schools. Nieto, also the editor of **What Keeps Teachers Going** ( Teachers College Press, 2003), believes that these twenty-one educators represent the "discourse of possibility" for a system plagued by daunting problems. These range from growing student diversity to legislative mandates for standards and accountability. These issues seem to have taken away from the original intention of public schools—an equal opportunity for all children. Nieto believes that the gap can be closed by recruiting, encouraging, and retaining teachers like the ones portrayed here.

Besides a preface, introduction, and conclusion written by the editor the middle of the book contains four sections, divided by themes: the path to teaching, how teaching helps teachers understand the world, how teachers help students find their place in the world, and how teaching helps them become more human. A brief explanation introduces the section's theme, and a bio of each teacher is provided before his or her essay. The essays are a wonderful mixture of insight, frustration, passion, struggle, and humor. They demonstrate a sense of mission and empathy for students, two of several qualities identified by Nieto as common to successful teachers. Their words reveal why—in spite of bureaucracy and low pay—they continue to teach. This book should be required reading for college students planning to enter the profession. Teachers already in the classroom, whether for five years or twenty-five, will be encouraged and inspired.—Kim Zack.

Willard, Nancy E. **Cyberbullying and Cyberthreats: Responding to the Challenge of Online Social Aggression, Threats**. Research Press, 2007. 320p. $38.95 Trade pb. 978-0-87822-537-8. VOYA June 2007.

There are three types of bullies including the social climber, and the three types of targets include the resilient target. There are also several types of cyberbullying, including synchronous and asynchronous. Six types of rationalizations allow students to justify why cyberbullying is okay. Everything one needs to know about cyberbullying is in this book. Williard's presentation is direct, clear, well documented, and without insider's jargon. One of the most helpful steps is the way Williard takes the reader from bullying to cyberbullying. Many unaware readers need the background that defines bullying before accessing the new information about cyberbullying. Others will appreciate the parallels between the two.

This book is incredibly complete. Besides the informative chapters, there are chapter reference notes and appendixes that provide everything that a school needs to create and implement a plan to address this problem from initial needs assessments for students and staff to use policies to guides for parents as well as students. There is nothing left out here except what is being discovered daily. There is no excess in this superbly written and much-needed professional text. If there is a child and a computer in one's life, it is a necessary read.—C.J. Bott.

A highlight of Williard's text is her overview, in chapter 2, of the technologies that teens and adults use that provide opportunities for cyberbullying. She covers traditional communications technologies (including email, chat and text messaging) and peer-to-peer networking and gaming. In the same chapter, Williard also provides a useful overview of what teens need to do to create an online profile.

This overview is the only section of the text where Williard describes specific technologies. Throughout the volume, however, she inserts information about technologies teens use to communicate and in this way demonstrates that cyberbullying is not completely separate from regular old-fashioned playground type bullying. The ultimate message is that with or without technology bullying is bullying. No matter what form bullying takes, children and teens need to be educated about why it is not a good thing.—Linda W. Braun, **VOYA** *Tag Team Tech* columnist.

Wiseman, Rosalind. **Owning Up Curriculum: Empowering Adolescents to Confront Social Cruelty, Bullying, and Injustice**. Research Press, 2009. 440p. $64.95 Trade pb., with CD. 978-0-87822-609-2. Further Reading. **VOYA** August 2009.

This reviewer had high expectations of Wiseman, whose other books, **Queen Bees and Wannabes** and **Queen Bee Moms and Kingpin Dads**, were stellar reads. Wiseman does not disappoint. She offers a curriculum to enable teens to combat bullying behaviors and their concomitant social challenges. Primary to understanding the curriculum is the strategy SEAL (social and emotional aspects of learning), which enables a person in a difficult situation to evaluate that moment, identify one's feelings, validate one's rights in that situation, and finally decide how to resolve the situation and move on. The use of SEAL is reinforced throughout the book. The curriculum suggests that the first six sessions should be taught in order and with single gender groups. Sessions seven through seventeen can be presented to the two genders together. In fact several of the boys' sessions are simply duplication of the same sessions in the girls' section. Every session is another look at one's place in what can often be a very confusing world. Especially favorite sessions are What's Up with Guys for girls and the boys' parallel, What's Up with Girls, as well as those covering the heavier topics of sexual harassment, cyberbullying, and abusive relationships. The book ends with a valuable resource section and a CD containing the forms and handouts.

Wiseman avoids the buzz word "bully." In a behavior curriculum, one cannot avoid the problem of bullying, but Wiseman weaves in so many issues, bullying is simply one of the many concerns discussed. Moving through the seventeen sessions over an extended time will help create a more accepting and supportive school environment that will benefit these children's lives in more ways than can be measured.—C. J. Bott.

Young Adult Library Services Association and Patrick Jones. **New Directions for**

**Library Service to Young Adults**. ALA Editions, 2002. 146p. $35 Trade pb. 978-0-8389-0827-3. Index. Biblio. Charts. Appendix. **VOYA** October 2002.

Clearly the best examination of libraries and teenagers to be published recently, this manual aims to "provide direction on how to establish quality library service to young adults in school and public libraries based upon the foundations of developmental needs, developmental assets, and youth development." Rather than emphasizing what is good for the library, it places library services to teens squarely in a developmental, community and collaborative context aimed at helping young adults thrive and grow into competent, caring adults. The content covers guidelines on planning, implementing, and evaluating services with youth involved in each step of the process. Twelve goal statements for YA services and ten core values upon which these goals are built are presented. The methods of reaching these goals are integrated with the American Library Association's two most relevant library divisions through the Public Library Association's **New Planning for Results: A Streamlined Approach** (Nelson, 2001) and the American Association of School Librarian's **Information Power: Building Partnerships for Learning** (AASL, 1998).

Jones supplies checklists of resources that can allocated for YA services from the categories of seven action areas common to libraries in almost any setting: administration, collections, programs, services, electronic resources, facilities and hours, and staff. A sixth chapter shares success stories from people who have used this approach all over the country in both school and public libraries. The last chapter lists possible outcomes for the library, such as positioning as a major youth-serving organization in the community; for the young adults, including feeling a part of something larger than themselves; and for the community, such as involving a large segment of their population in their discussion and decision making, which adds to the richness of civic dialogue. Ten appendixes cover everything from competencies for staff who serve teens to guidelines for youth participation.

Besides his usual clear writing, ubiquitous lists, and deft editorial organization, Jones writes a manifesto for how services for young adults should be conceptualized. Far surpassing its YALSA predecessors and even his own **Connecting Young Adults and Libraries** (Neal-Schumann, 1998/**VOYA** August 1998), this is THE book that every YA and secondary school librarian should have handy. Unlike all the "how-to-do-it-good cookbooks" abounding in library literature, this one is about "how-to-think-it-good" and serves as a model for services conceptualization for the adolescent age group. – Mary K. Chelton.

**Youth, Pornography, and the Internet: Can We Provide Sound Choices in a Safe Environment?** Committee to Study Tools and Strategies for Protecting Kids from Pornography and Their Applicability to Other Inappropriate Internet Content, Eds. National Academy Press, 2002. 424p. $47.95 Trade pb. 978-0-309-08274-7. Glossary. Index. Appendix. **VOYA** February 2003.

This report, which is also available online at http://www.nap.edu, summarizes the findings, conclusions, and recommendations of a distinguished committee selected by the National Research Council (NRC), part of the National Academy of Sciences, in response to Title IX, Section 901 of Public Law 105-314, the Protection of Children from

Sexual Predators Act of 1998, passed by the United States Congress. Headed by then Attorney General Dick Thornburgh, the NRC group was charged to seek "to frame the problem of [computer transmission of pornographic images] in an appropriate social, legal, educational, technological, and ethical context; present what is and is not scientifically known about the impact on children of exposure to sexually explicit materials; and provide information useful to various decision-making communities about possible courses of action across educational, legislative, law enforcement, and technological fronts." The committee held hearings, called for white papers that are posted on http://www.itasnrc.org, and reviewed other studies. The final report emphasizes approaches to protecting youth from material deemed inappropriate for minors, with no consensus by the committee that inappropriate sexually explicit material is the most important safety issue on the Internet for children. The report is divided into three parts. Part I includes an introduction, chapters on technology that explain cyberspace and the Internet; the adult entertainment industry, with the interesting statistic that 20 to 30 percent of the material on those adult sites goes to children; the legal and regulatory issues surrounding Internet use and regulation, specifically the First Amendment and obscenity legislation plus international dimensions; how children use media and are exposed to sexually explicit material; the research base on the impact of such exposure, and various perspectives on the public debate in the absence of a scientific consensus on impact. Part II discusses various strategies to protect youth from a discussion of "protection itself to educational or technological tools for users and non-end users." Part III summarizes the committee's findings, conclusions, and future needs, which in essence, say that too many competing goals and values inform the debate so that "any 'appropriate' mix of actions should be seen as balancing competing goals and values rather than endorsing he absolute supremacy of any one goal or value." This study is required reading for all youth-serving librarians.-Mary K. Chelton.

Zollo, Peter. **Getting Wiser to Teens: More Insights into Marketing to Teenagers**, 3rd Ed. New Strategist Publications, Inc. (P. O. Box 242, Ithaca, NY 14851), 2004. 424p. $54.95. 978-1-885070-54-8. *The View from VOYA*, **VOYA August 2004.**

When VOYA reviewed **Wise Up to Teens: Insights into Marketing and Advertising to Teenagers** (1995/VOYA August 1996), young adult librarians were delighted to discover a related field with so much useful information about teens. Libraries market services to teens much as businesses target teens as customers.

The third edition of Zollo's indispensable guide especially merits VOYA readers' attention, for the world of teen marketing has morphed into unprecedented savvy on both sides: those who court lucrative teen business, and the thirty-three million teens being courted. When Zollo co-founded his market research firm, Teen Research Unlimited (TRU) in 1982 (just four years after VOYA debuted), no other research focused exclusively on teens. TRU interviewed more than a half a million teens. Getting Wiser to Teens distills the findings into valuable views into teen psyches, attitudes, trends, and behaviors.

Zollo's respect for and understanding of teens is obvious in his lively, well-organized text that analyzes loads of statistics in a readable manner. His social-marketing efforts in the antitobacco and antidrug movements reveal his commitment to teens' well-being.

Zollo identifies five fundamental teen needs for fun, independence, indi-filiation—a TRU-coined word for the hybrid of individuality and affiliation—experimentation, and aspiration. He coherently resolves ambiguities in teens' natures in discussions of conformity/nonconformity and peer pressure, which "stems from internal desires rather than external pressures from friends."

Because Zollo respects teens' opinions, librarians selling services and information will recognize him as one of us. "All teen marketing efforts should have at their underpinnings the objective of solving this age group's problems and/or addressing its needs," he concludes. "Our role is to include the consumer in the marketing process. We advocate for teens on a daily basis to assure that their voices are heard loudly and clearly."—Catherine Dunn MacRae.

# Index

CPSIA information can be obtained at www.ICGtesting.com
Printed in the USA
BVOW051915030613

322316BV00002B/2/P

9 781617 510106